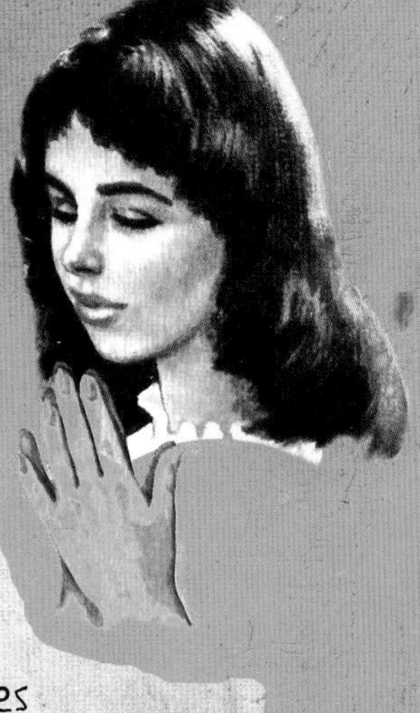

Ericka

Ericka is one of the missing, and her mother keeps her bedroom perfectly preserved. I'm standing in the doorway, my ears ringing from the silence. Sunlight catches dust particles. Ericka's mother dusts the bedroom every day, and washes the linens regularly. She tells me that although she works as a cleaning lady in an office building, she still likes to clean. I can see it in her hands: They are scraped and raw, peeling from cleaning chemicals. The ammonia in here makes me dizzy, yet to Ericka's mother, it seems that there is something comforting and familiar in this smell. I think I can understand this.

My grandmother on my father's side used to go to the hairdresser once a week, chauffeured by my grandfather in his Cadillac. She would come back with her hair frosted blond, sculpted wide and high. She was just so glamorous in her gold earrings and pink lipstick. Could she possibly be the most sophisticated woman that I had ever seen? Her apartment was scoured clean, smelling like ammonia. Her plastic-covered couch was always shiny, her collection of porcelain figurines - blushing ladies holding parasols next to small dogs - endlessly fascinating. Somehow, they began to represent what I hoped to be my entire family's future: blond, unfettered, and pure.

Sometimes, though, my grandmother would cry. At unexpected times, like when she was polishing the couch. It made me feel naked and wobbly. At the time, she was incomprehensible.

Her caricature, her television, and that's her red bandana sticking out.

Su caricatura, su
television se asoma
U pañuelo rojo que usaba

The place where I washed her feet so she could rest.

Lugar donde me
lababa los pies paraque
descansara

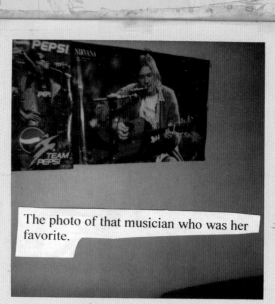

The photo of that musician who was her favorite.

La foto de este
artista que era
su favorito los

This is where I said goodbye to Ericka the day that she left.

En este Lugar
despedi a Ericka
el dia que se fué

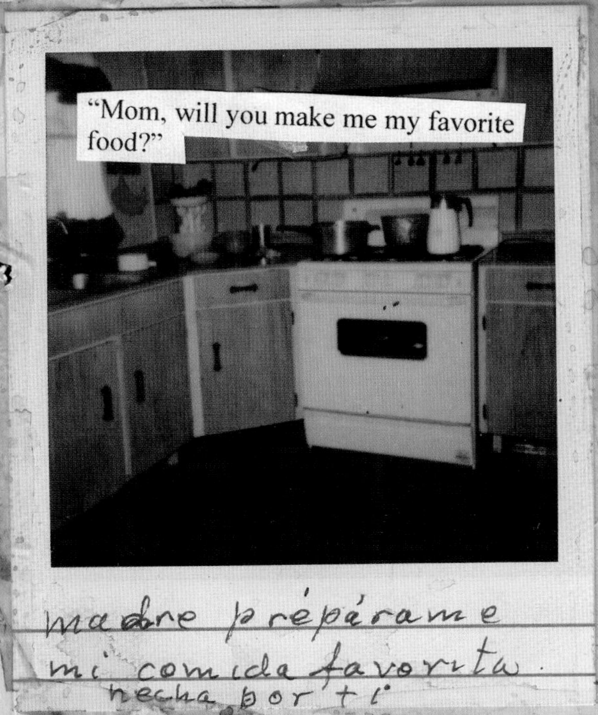
"Mom, will you make me my favorite food?"
madre prépárame
mi comida favorita
hecha por ti

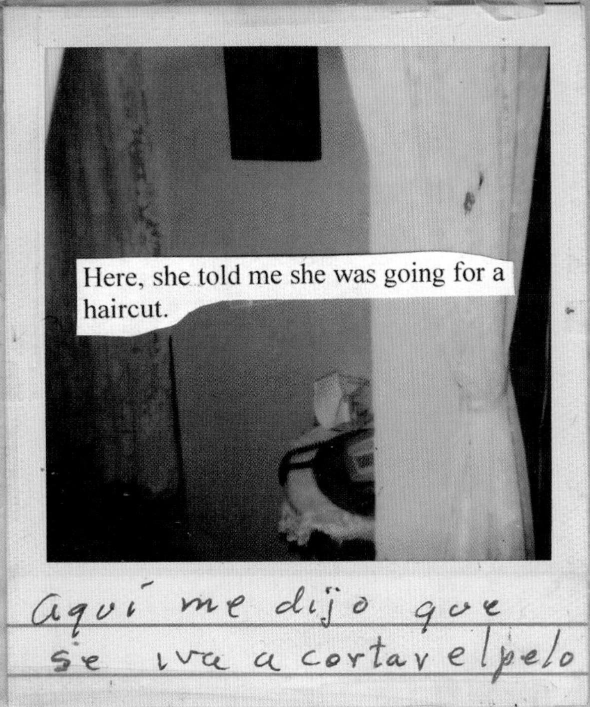
Here, she told me she was going for a haircut.
aquí me dijo que
se iva a cortar el pelo

Ericka's mother begins to take pictures for me. Polaroids. Her table, her couch, her bedroom wall, her front steps, her plants... in the space below each photo, she writes about all of the things that she and her daughter used to do. Each photograph is thoughtful and considered, as though in these empty spaces she is giving her love, and receiving her daughter's in return. Later, we go to the highway where she first looked for Ericka after she went missing. The images become vague. Portraits of dirt. We go to the mall where her daughter had gone for a haircut and was never seen again. The last few pictures are blurry. Her hand must have been shaking.

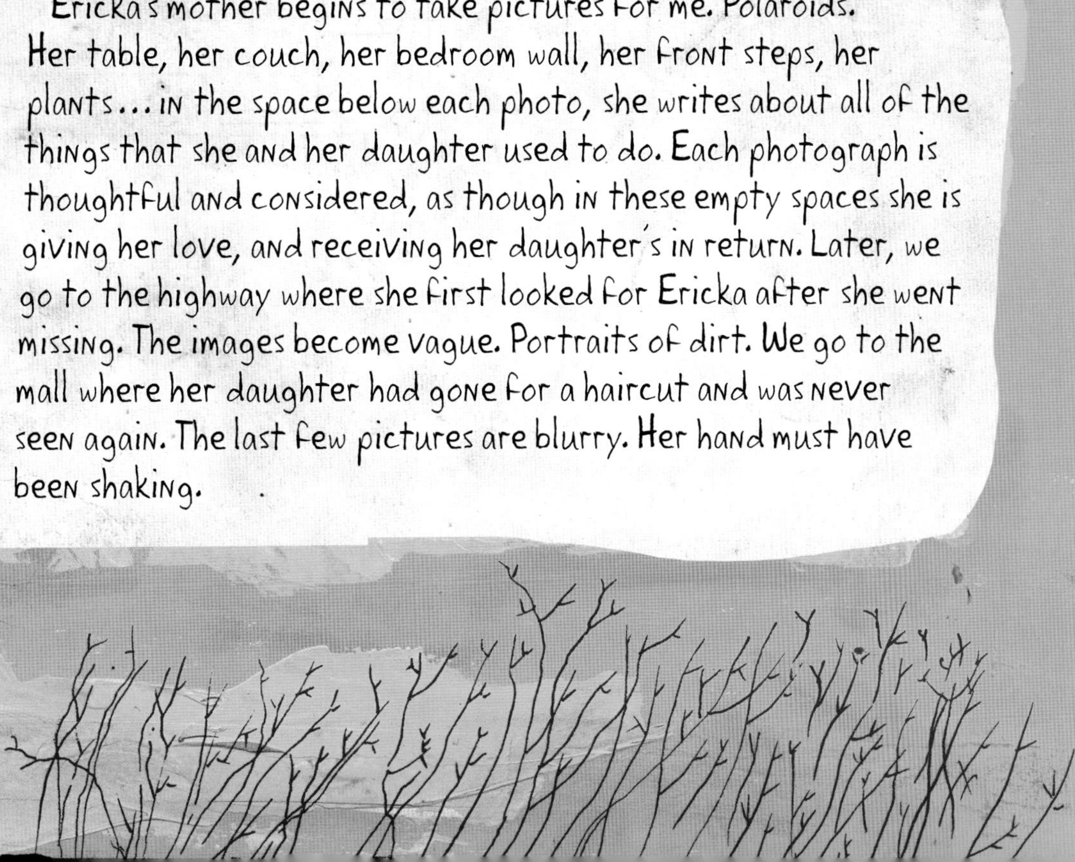

I have three manila folders filled with research on these murders. None of it can explain why the killer or killers haven't been found. Juárez sits on an international border that is lined with some of the most sophisticated surveillance and crime-fighting operations in the world. Billions of dollars in trade change hands here every year. How is it possible that no one can find the money or resources to solve the murders of all these young women? I ask the same question to my translator, a young woman from Juárez, as we drive in a Toyota that smells like eggs and plastic.

"I don't know," she says, and changes the radio station again from music to commercials.

We pull into the parking lot of the 7-Eleven for lunch. The translator and I don't talk much. Today, during an interview with the mother of a murdered girl, the translator began to cry and left the room. I followed, hugged her, and told her that I find the stories upsetting as well. She gave me this look, like "dumb-ass," and said she was just hungry, couldn't I see that we had worked through her break and she needed to eat? And anyway, whatever, she's heard this story before.

Mostly when we do talk it's about the Backstreet Boys. We both like one of their songs: "As Long as You Love Me."

Later, in my hotel room, I study pictures of the missing and murdered girls. They're between the ages of 14 and 18. Thin, with long dark hair. They look like girls who might have had their lockers next to mine at Oakwood Collegiate. The ones who shared Finesse hair spray as they teased their bangs in a mirror, talking about their first kiss in the basement at a house party, trading secrets about the boy they had a huge crush on OH MY GOD THERE HE IS HE'S WALKING PAST YOUR LOCKER DID HE LOOK AT ME? Girls making late-night phone calls, acting older, skipping school to get a second ear piercing, swearing forever pacts with best friends, wanting to be smarter, to get along with their mothers, trying to be better.

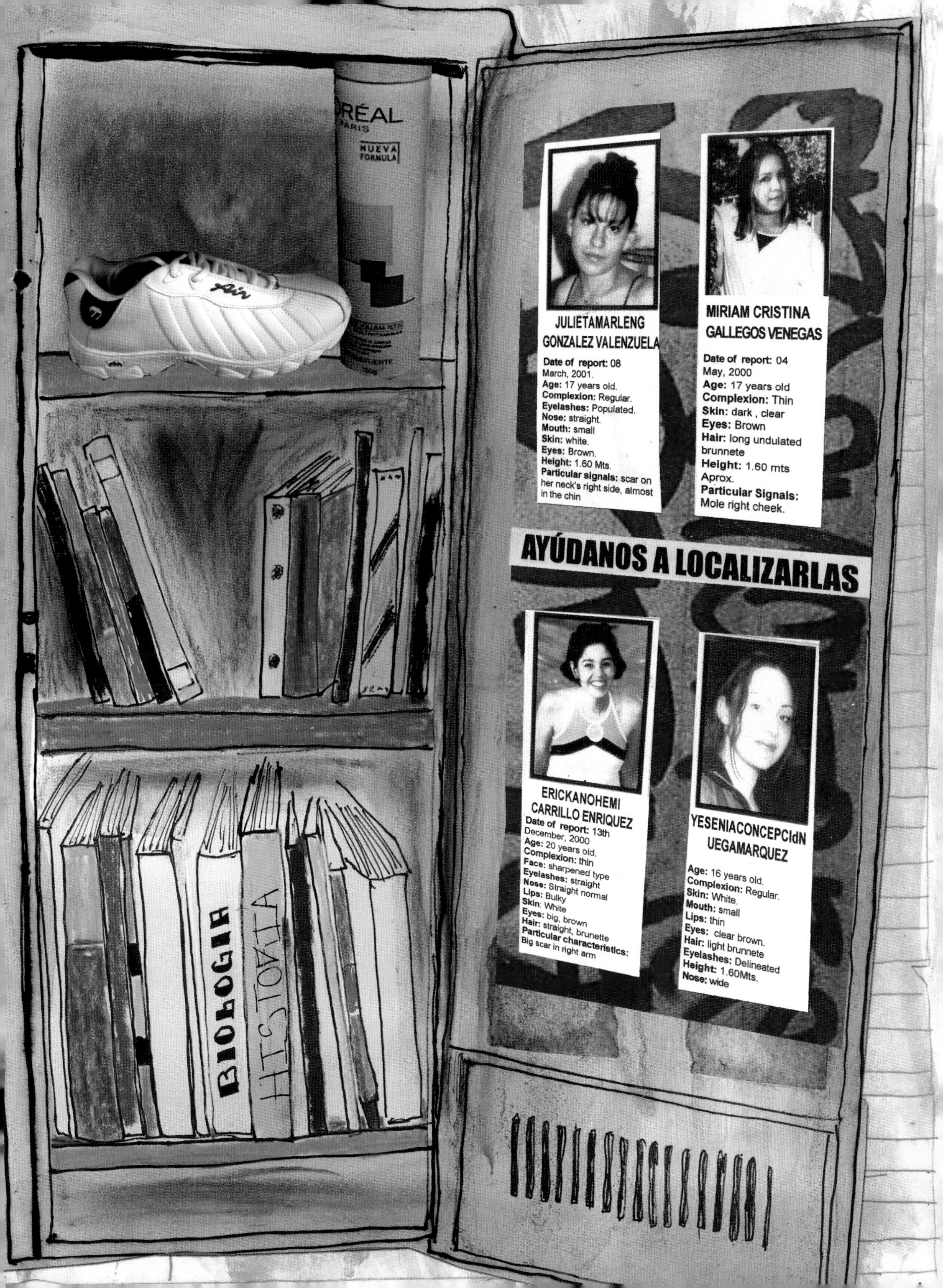

L'ORÉAL
PARIS
NUEVA FORMULA
JULIETAMARLENG
GONZALEZ VALENZUELA
Date of report: 08 March, 2001.
Age: 17 years old.
Complexion: Regular.
Eyelashes: Populated.
Nose: straight.
Mouth: small
Skin: white.
Eyes: Brown.
Height: 1.60 Mts.
Particular signals: scar on her neck's right side, almost in the chin
MIRIAM CRISTINA
GALLEGOS VENEGAS
Date of report: 04 May, 2000
Age: 17 years old
Complexion: Thin
Skin: dark , clear
Eyes: Brown
Hair: long undulated brunnete
Height: 1.60 mts Aprox.
Particular Signals: Mole right cheek.
AYÚDANOS A LOCALIZARLAS
ERICKANOHEMI
CARRILLO ENRIQUEZ
Date of report: 13th December, 2000
Age: 20 years old.
Complexion: thin
Face: sharpened type
Eyelashes: straight
Nose: Straight normal
Lips: Bulky
Skin: White
Eyes: big, brown
Hair: straight, brunette
Particular characteristics: Big scar in right arm
YESENIACONCEPCIdN
UEGAMARQUEZ
Age: 16 years old.
Complexion: Regular.
Skin: White.
Mouth: small
Lips: thin
Eyes: clear brown.
Hair: light brunnete
Eyelashes: Delineated
Height: 1.60Mts.
Nose: wide
BIOLOGIA
HISTORIA

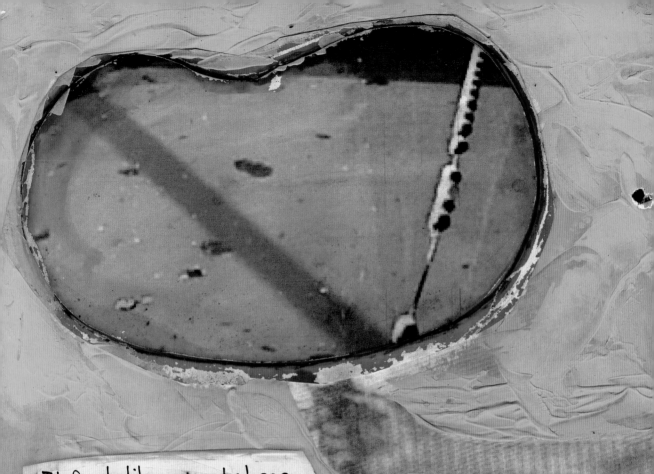

It feels like secrets here, bottled up and buried in earth.

At first, I didn't know why. Blank ribbons of highway unfurled as a taxi took me from El Paso, Texas, into Ciudad Juárez. Through the window, endless roadside strip malls flickered past. A bridal shop, a bar fronted by a neon cactus. We sped by. By the time my taxi dropped me off at the Holiday Inn, I could taste sadness in my lime-flavored chips and Coke.

One month ago, in preparation for my trip, I attended a conference at UCLA. Over the course of two days, journalists, feminists, students, professors, and human rights workers gathered to discuss the murders that happen in Juárez. How could this be happening? What could be done? The seminars were dense and theoretical and well intentioned. The stories of the missing women and their families only came alive when the mothers took to the stage. One mother, who had fierce india-ink eyes and a slow voice, described her daughter's killing in a way that seemed ravaged. How many times had she repeated these details to an audience of strangers? I imagined it was an act that felt like suffocation.

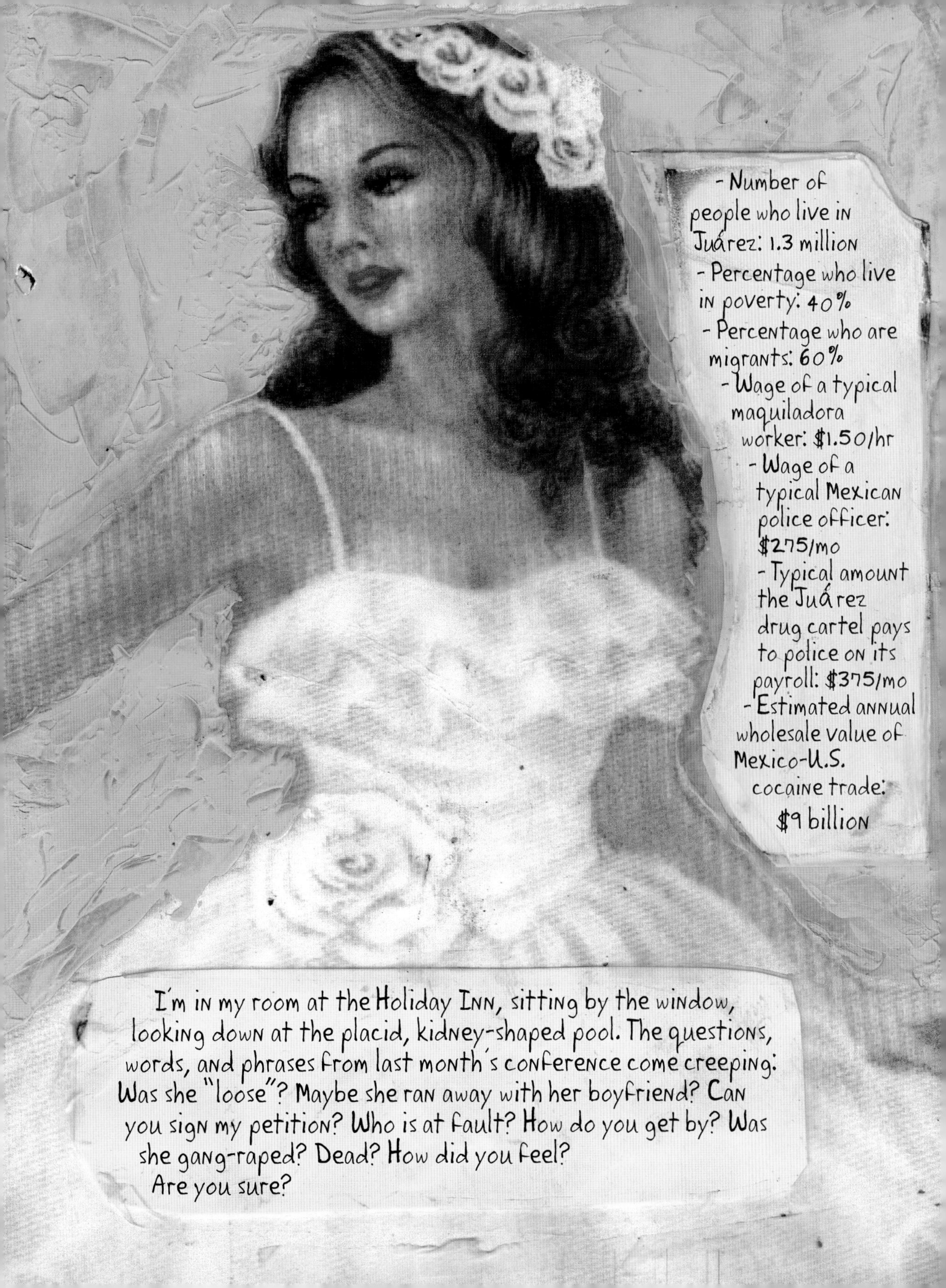
- Number of people who live in Juárez: 1.3 million
- Percentage who live in poverty: 40%
- Percentage who are migrants: 60%
- Wage of a typical maquiladora worker: $1.50/hr
- Wage of a typical Mexican police officer: $275/mo
- Typical amount the Juárez drug cartel pays to police on its payroll: $375/mo
- Estimated annual wholesale value of Mexico-U.S. cocaine trade: $9 billion
I'm in my room at the Holiday Inn, sitting by the window, looking down at the placid, kidney-shaped pool. The questions, words, and phrases from last month's conference come creeping: Was she "loose"? Maybe she ran away with her boyfriend? Can you sign my petition? Who is at fault? How do you get by? Was she gang-raped? Dead? How did you feel? Are you sure?

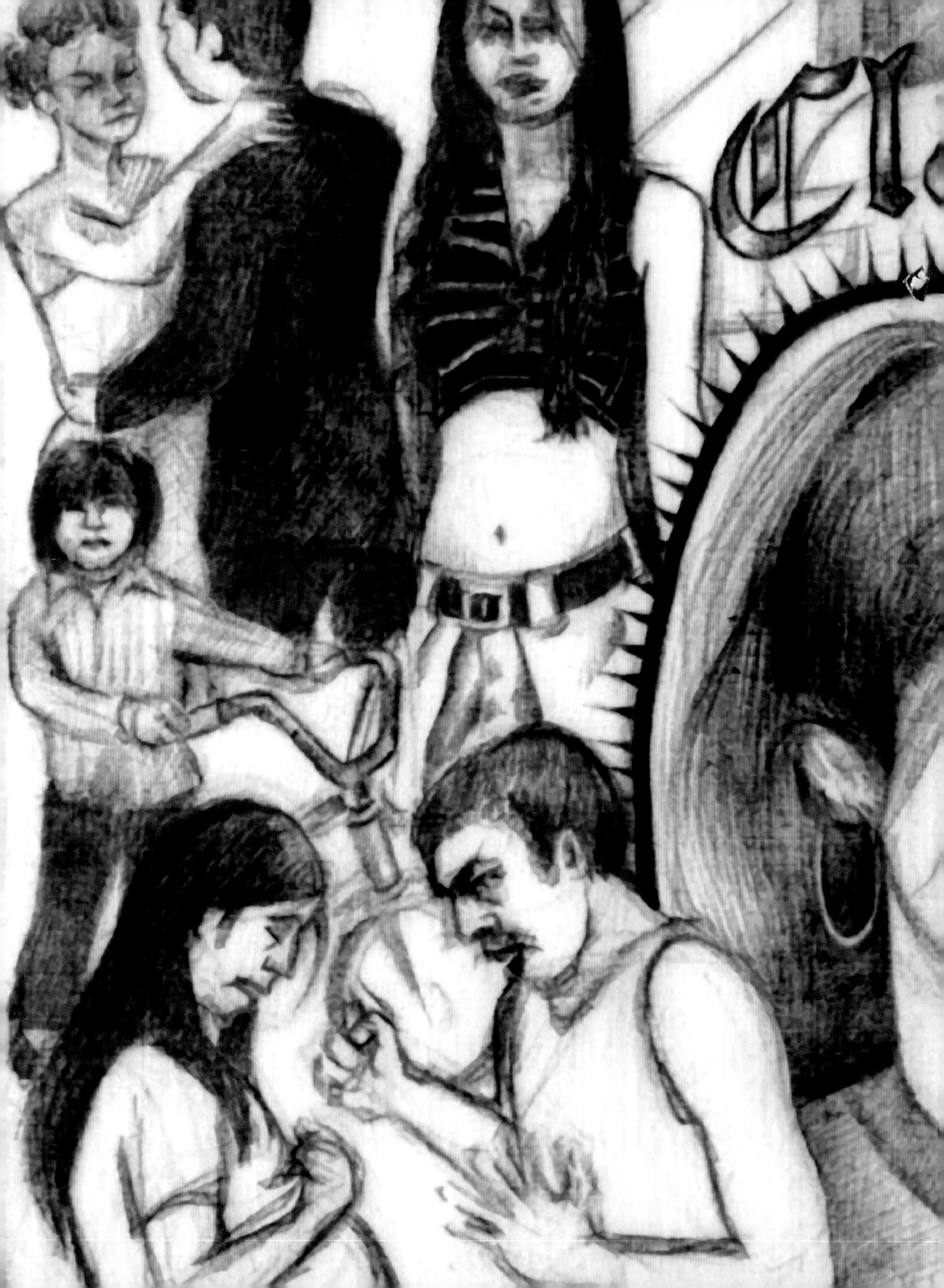

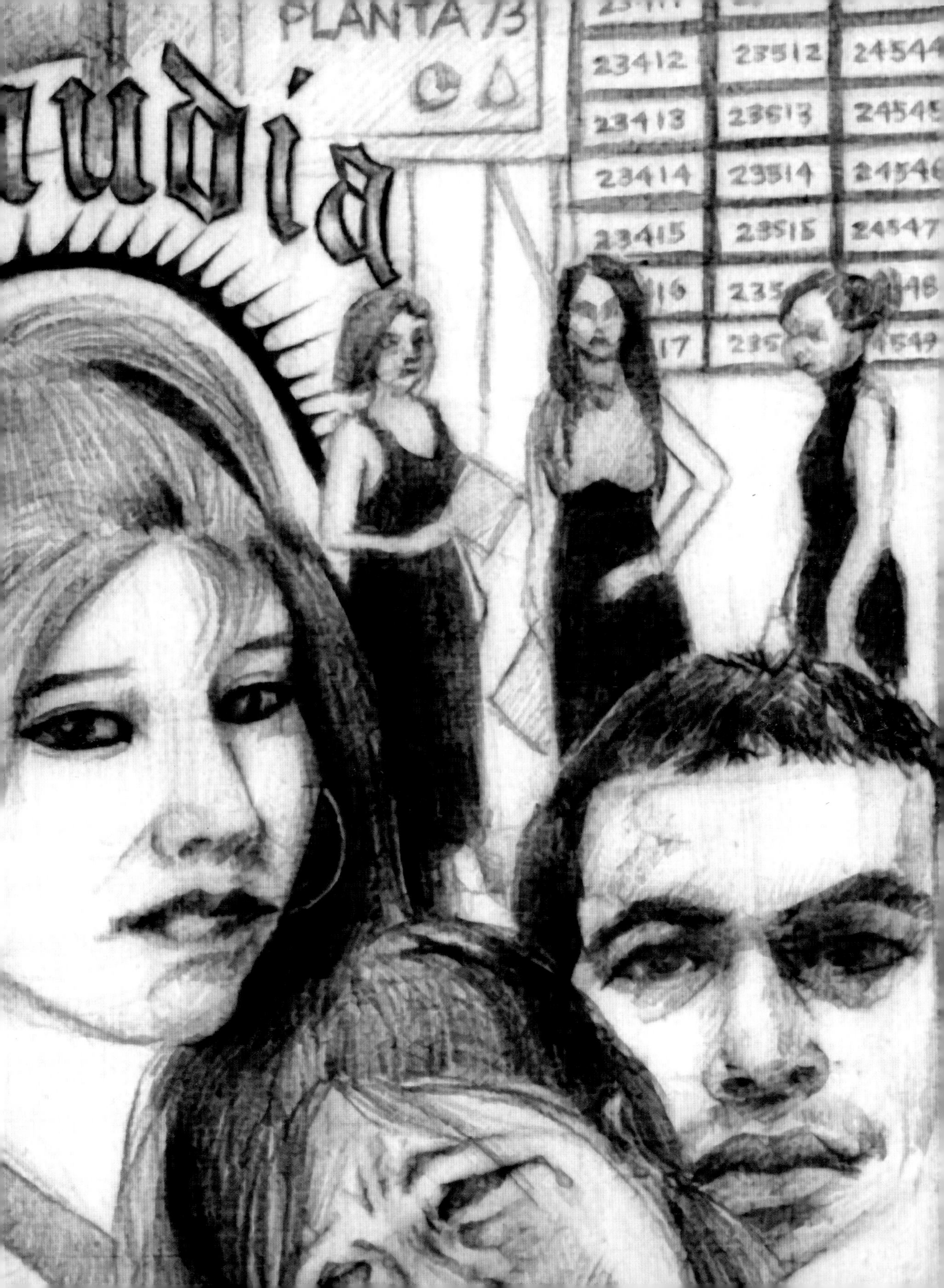
PLANTA 13
23412
23512
24544
23413
23513
24545
23414
23514
24546
23415
23515
24547

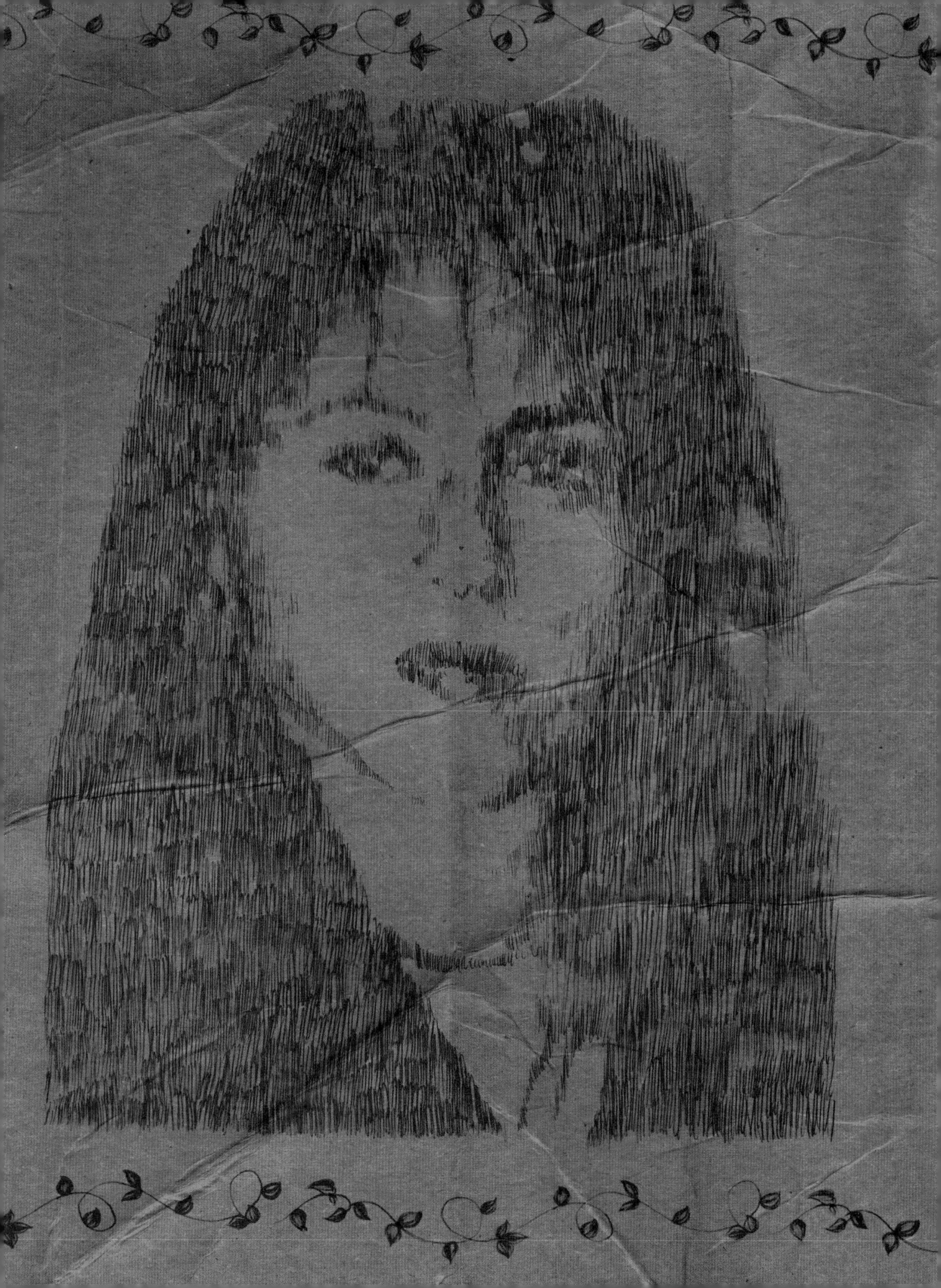

Twenty poems

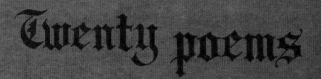

Claudia, you came into my life last summer in a twenty-five-kilogram FedEx box. I carried it up to my bedroom and shut the door. There was no music, no sound from outside. I took my penknife, slit a line in the top of that box, and opened it carefully, peeling back the cardboard. Inside were notes by your family and friends. There were photos of a place where the sun hangs low and hungry between plumes of industrial smoke. There were the missing-person posters: Claudia Ivette González, age twenty. Pale skin, brown eyes, light brown hair.

I was thinking how the only time I ever went to Mexico, I sat on a beach in Puerto Vallarta and later bought a papier-mâché puppet at the marketplace. I got home, took it out of my suitcase, and the strings were all tangled. There was nothing to do but throw it out.

about Claudia

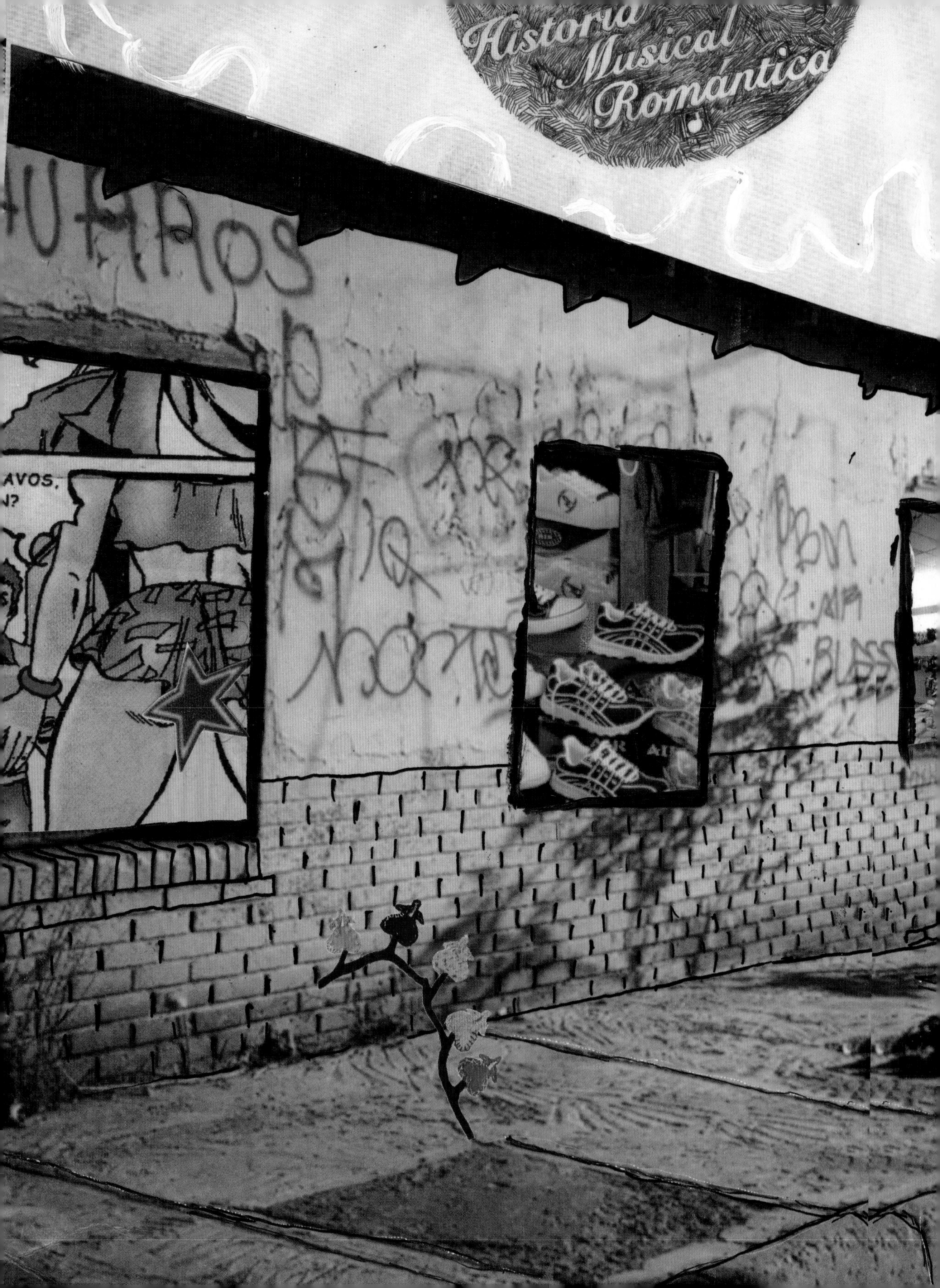
Historia Musical Romántica

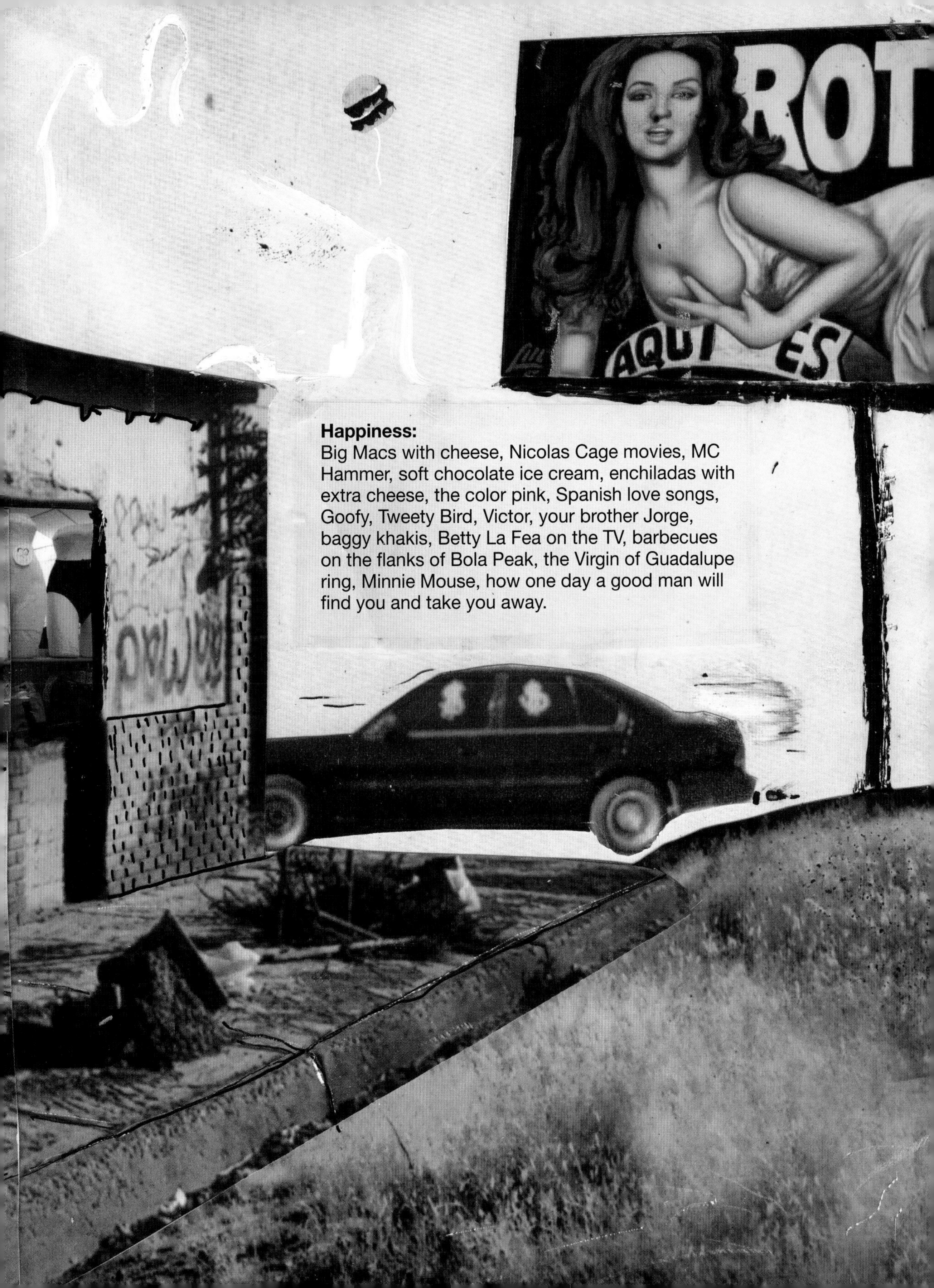
ROT
AQUI
ES

Happiness:
Big Macs with cheese, Nicolas Cage movies, MC Hammer, soft chocolate ice cream, enchiladas with extra cheese, the color pink, Spanish love songs, Goofy, Tweety Bird, Victor, your brother Jorge, baggy khakis, Betty La Fea on the TV, barbecues on the flanks of Bola Peak, the Virgin of Guadalupe ring, Minnie Mouse, how one day a good man will find you and take you away.

It is hours past dusk, and a white-painted bus snakes through a town that is falling asleep. A girl, twenty years old and a little stooped, sits near the front, watching the road. She passes Wal-Marts, Blockbusters, shopping malls, black-tinted cars, girls with waxed eyebrows and brown lipstick. Men sniffing glue from brown paper bags, eleven-year-olds still in their checkered school uniforms. In the distance, huge factories puff the odor of metal and fire. A sign on a clothing store: SÍ SE PUEDE. Yes, you can. On $55 U.S. dollars a week, you can buy half a pair of blue Guess sneakers or a beige denim jumper and white blouse with stripes. You can buy nine Big Mac meals or just a little less than one pair of American jeans with broncos on the label, made right here in Ciudad Juárez, the city of missing women. You can buy a swatch of fake, plum-red hair and pay the beautician on Avenida Juárez to take up her half-moon needle and sew it in. You can buy the hair of a beauty. *Sí se puede.* It can be done.

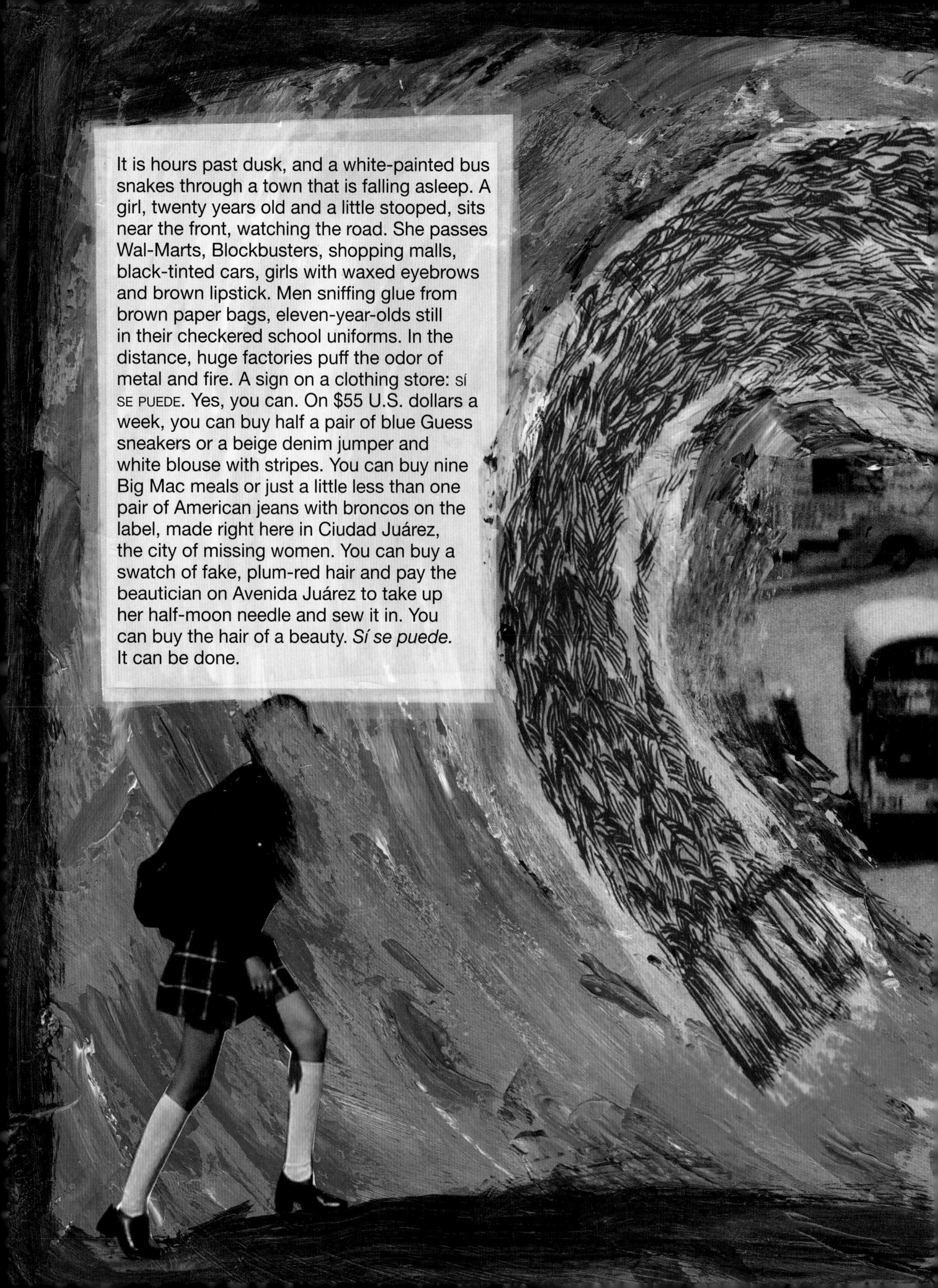

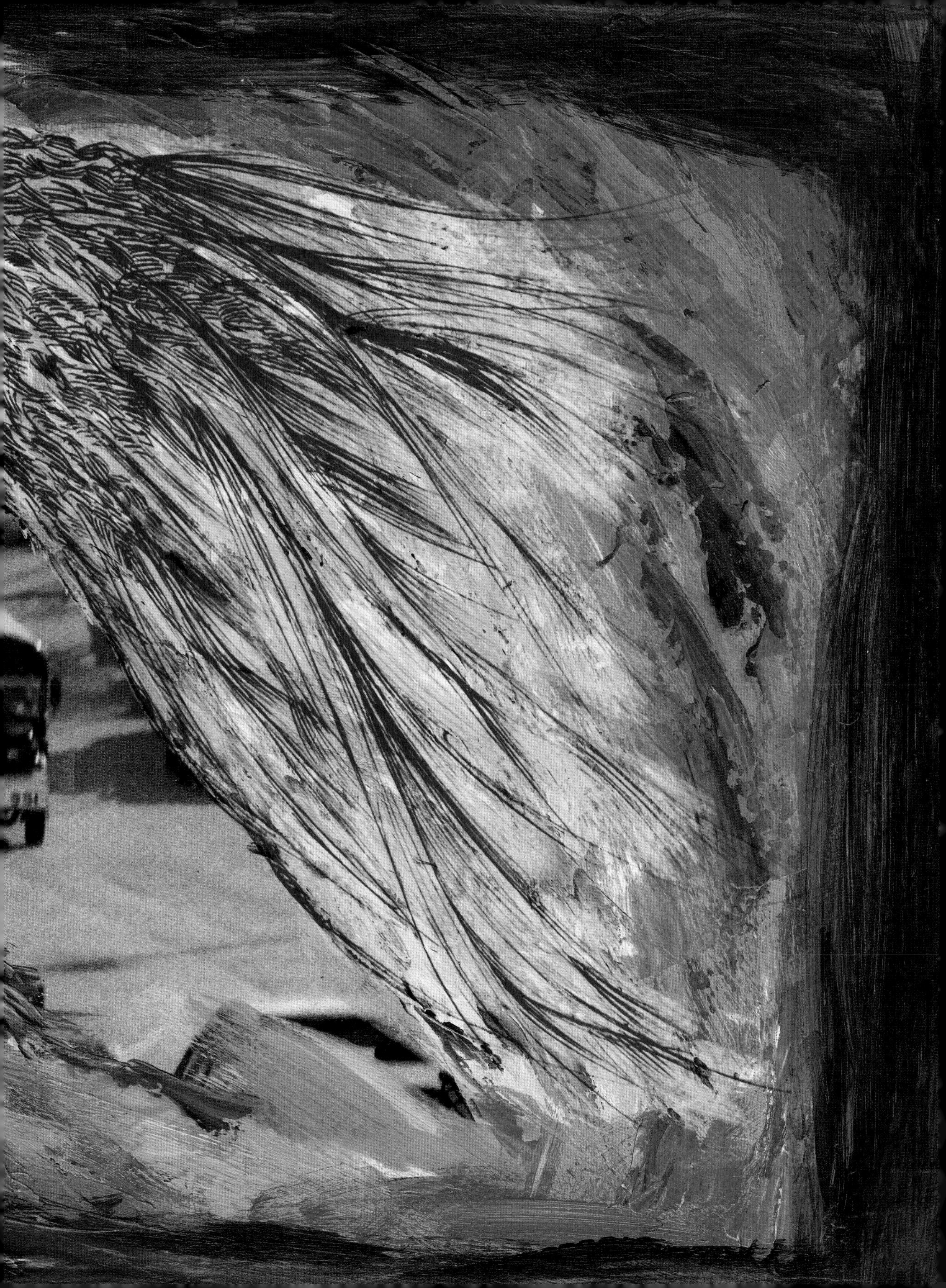

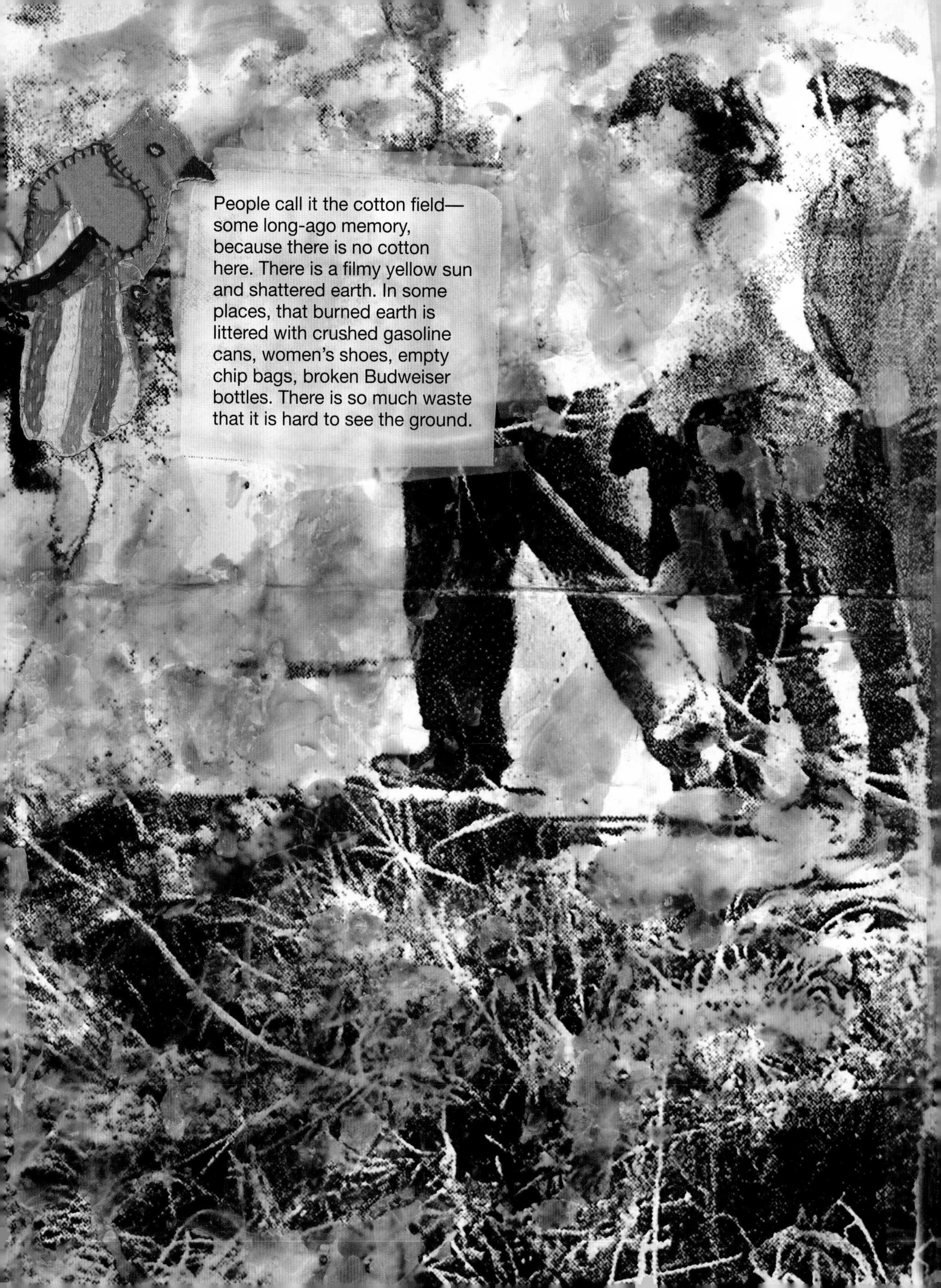

People call it the cotton field—some long-ago memory, because there is no cotton here. There is a filmy yellow sun and shattered earth. In some places, that burned earth is littered with crushed gasoline cans, women's shoes, empty chip bags, broken Budweiser bottles. There is so much waste that it is hard to see the ground.

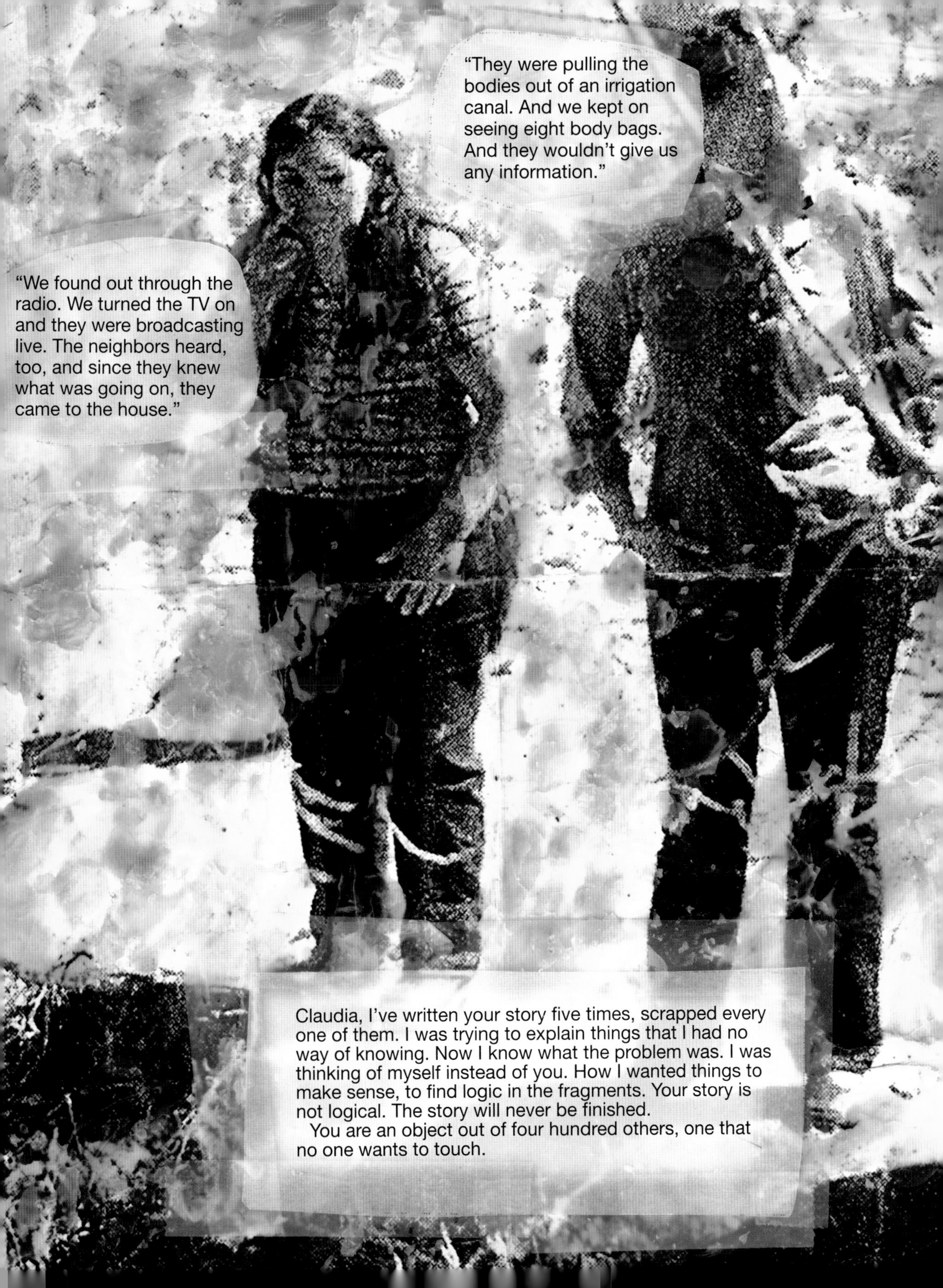
"They were pulling the bodies out of an irrigation canal. And we kept on seeing eight body bags. And they wouldn't give us any information."
"We found out through the radio. We turned the TV on and they were broadcasting live. The neighbors heard, too, and since they knew what was going on, they came to the house."

Claudia, I've written your story five times, scrapped every one of them. I was trying to explain things that I had no way of knowing. Now I know what the problem was. I was thinking of myself instead of you. How I wanted things to make sense, to find logic in the fragments. Your story is not logical. The story will never be finished.

You are an object out of four hundred others, one that no one wants to touch.

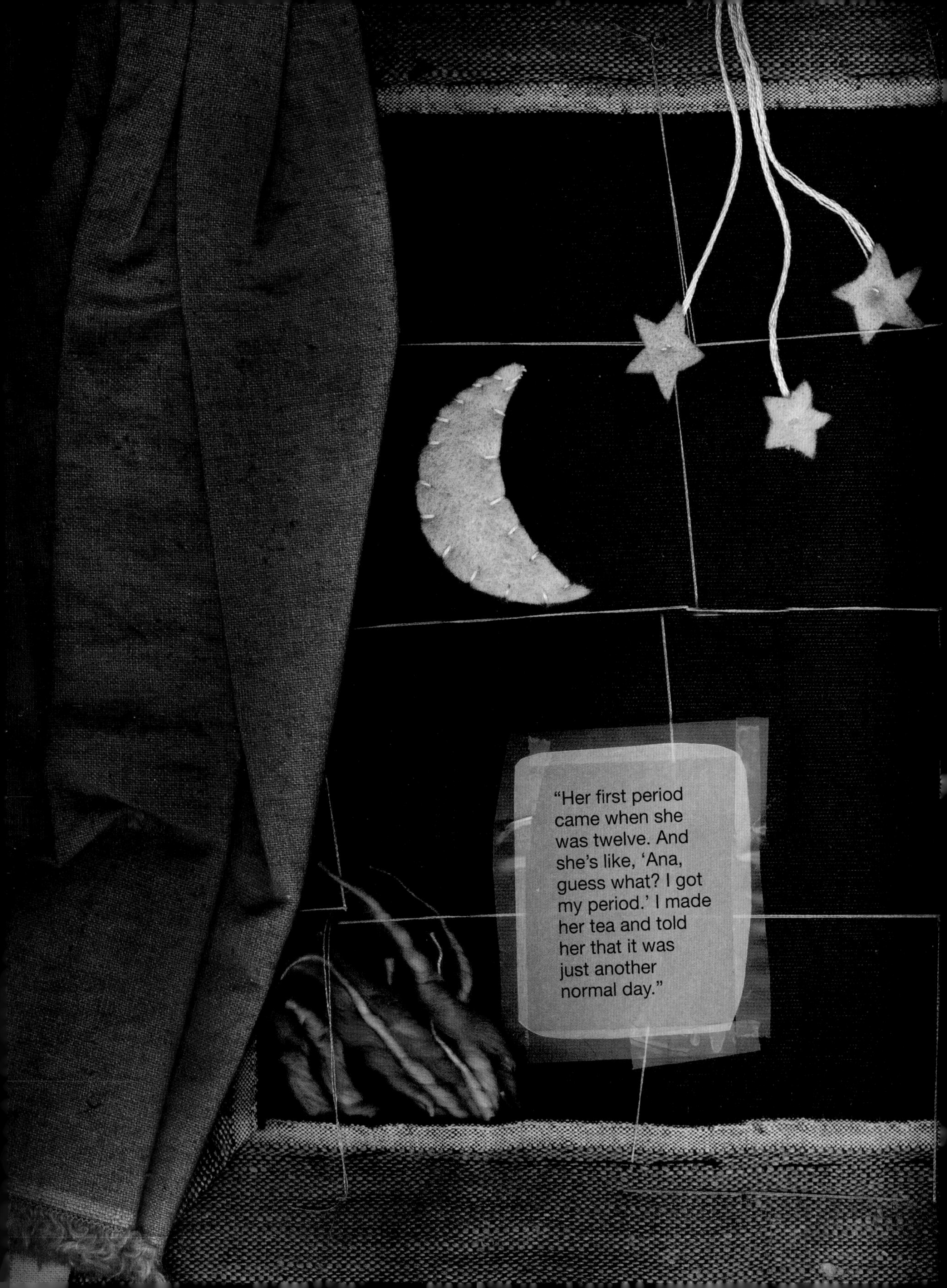
"Her first period came when she was twelve. And she's like, 'Ana, guess what? I got my period.' I made her tea and told her that it was just another normal day."

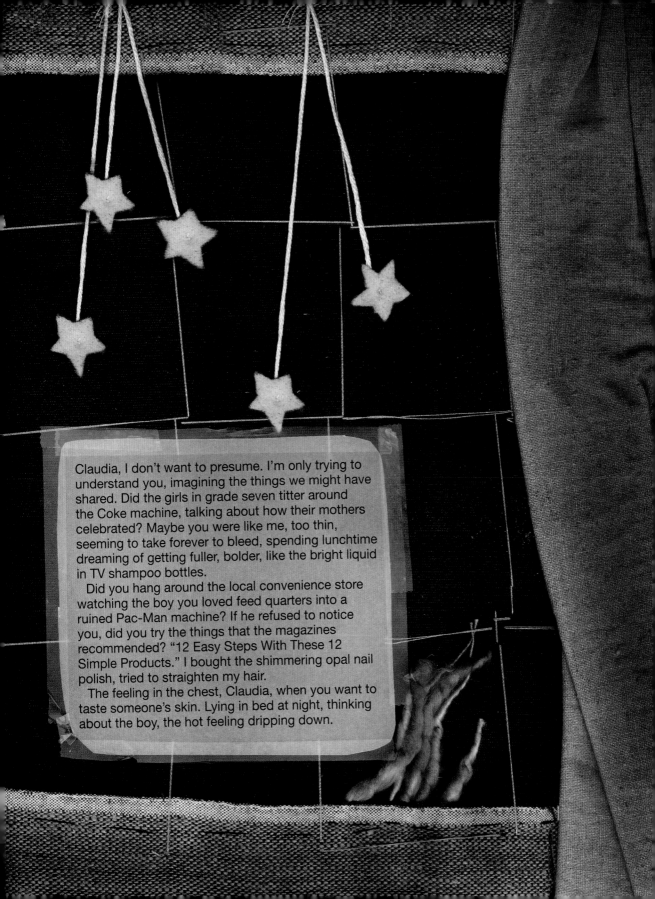

Claudia, I don't want to presume. I'm only trying to understand you, imagining the things we might have shared. Did the girls in grade seven titter around the Coke machine, talking about how their mothers celebrated? Maybe you were like me, too thin, seeming to take forever to bleed, spending lunchtime dreaming of getting fuller, bolder, like the bright liquid in TV shampoo bottles.

Did you hang around the local convenience store watching the boy you loved feed quarters into a ruined Pac-Man machine? If he refused to notice you, did you try the things that the magazines recommended? "12 Easy Steps With These 12 Simple Products." I bought the shimmering opal nail polish, tried to straighten my hair.

The feeling in the chest, Claudia, when you want to taste someone's skin. Lying in bed at night, thinking about the boy, the hot feeling dripping down.

Some of the men in Claudia's life:
– Her brother, Jorge, who is always smiling.
Nothing ever stops him.
– Jorge's father, who beat their mother and
then left her.
– Her sister Mayela's father. Their mother
met him at a dance hall, they fell in love,
and he gave her a daughter. Then he died
in a car crash.
– Troy Aikman, legendary quarterback of
the Dallas Cowboys.
– Her sister Gema's father, gone.
– Gema's boyfriend, in jail in America for
sexually abusing their nephew.
– Idet's boyfriend. Idet is Claudia's best
friend. Her boyfriend is in prison, and
Claudia helps buy diapers for Idet's baby.
– Snoop Dogg.
– Her own father, gone.

"My mother got these calls on her cell phone. Like four of them. And the people would be laughing and shit, and would say that they saw Claudia. They wouldn't give their names. They told me that she was downtown and real skinny. She was using and selling drugs and going crazy. She was shooting herself up. And this person knew my name. And this guy on the phone told me to go and look for her."

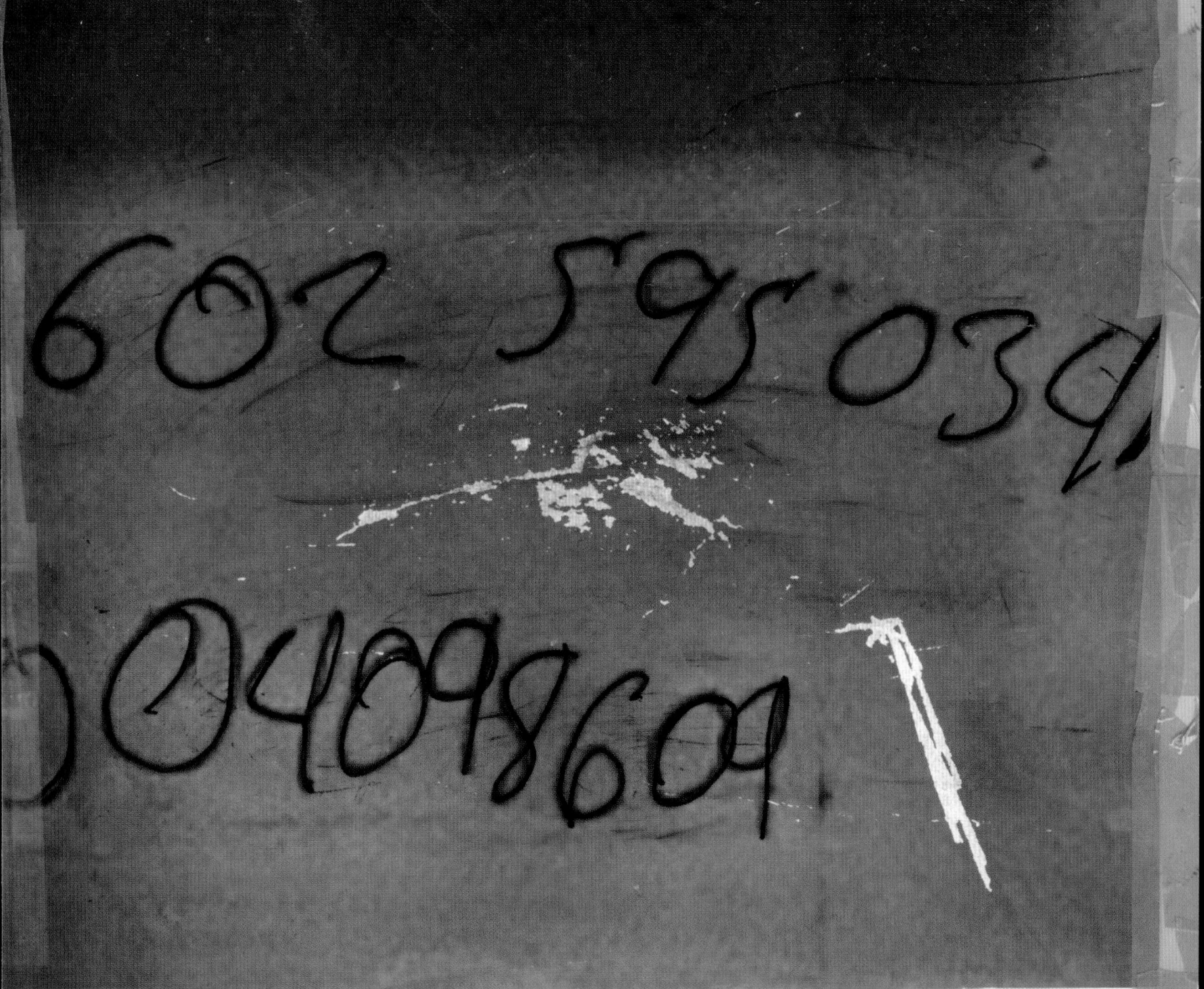

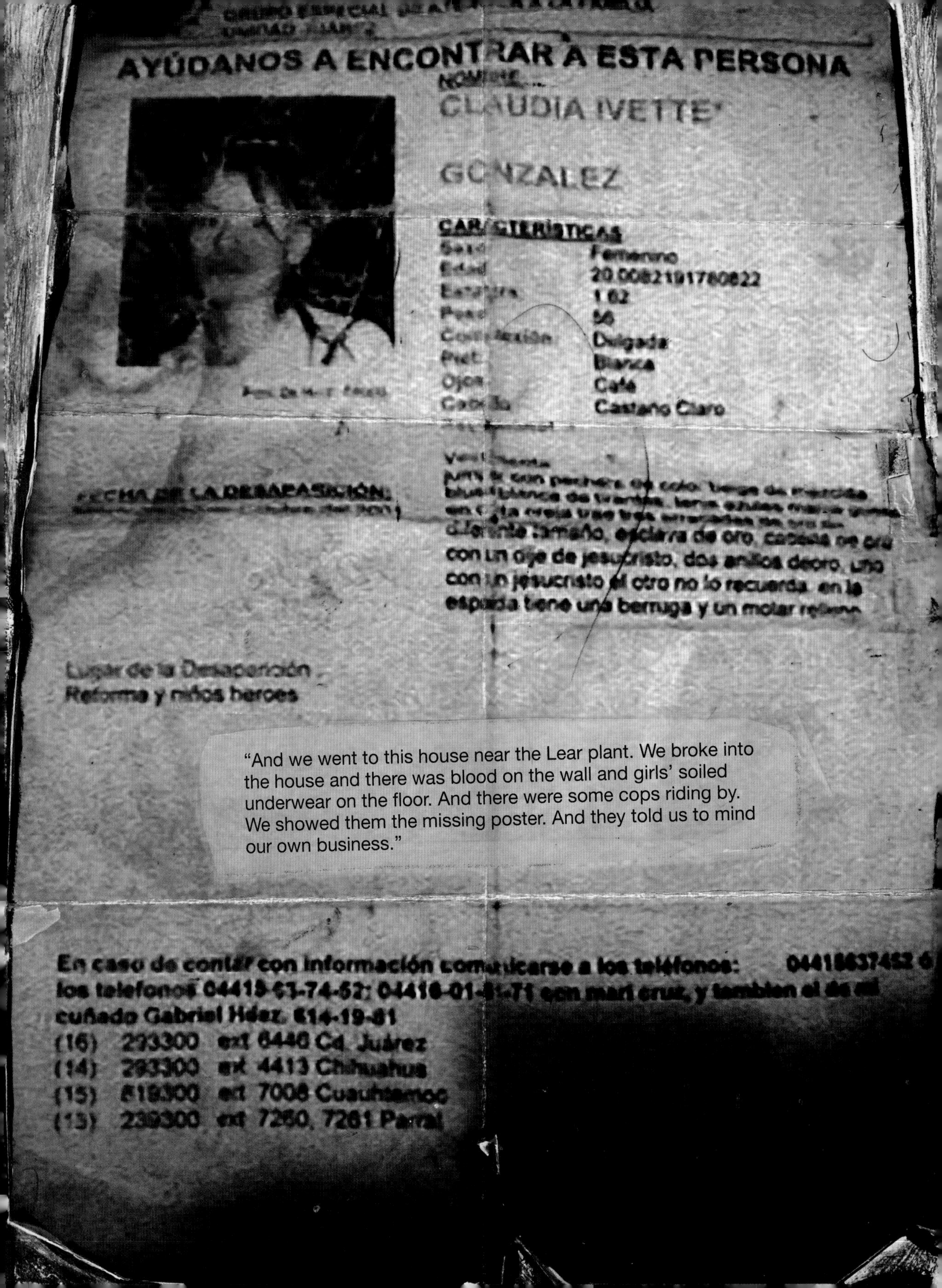

AYÚDANOS A ENCONTRAR A ESTA PERSONA

NOMBRE

CLAUDIA IVETTE

GONZALEZ

CARACTERÍSTICAS

Sexo	Femenino
Edad	20.0082191780822
Estatura	1.62
Peso	56
Complexión	Delgada
Piel	Blanca
Ojos	Café
Cabello	Castaño Claro

Vestimenta

MTV ... con pechera de color beige de mezcla blue blanca de tirantes, tenis adidas marca güera en ... la ceja trae tres aretadas en uno de diferente tamaño, esclava de oro, cadena de oro con un dije de jesucristo, dos anillos deoro, uno con un jesucristo el otro no lo recuerda, en la espalda tiene una berruga y un molar relleno.

FECHA DE LA DESAPARICIÓN:

Lugar de la Desaparición
Reforma y niños heroes

"And we went to this house near the Lear plant. We broke into the house and there was blood on the wall and girls' soiled underwear on the floor. And there were some cops riding by. We showed them the missing poster. And they told us to mind our own business."

En caso de contar con información comunicarse a los teléfonos: 04418637452 6
los telefonos 04413-63-74-52; 04416-01-81-71 con mari cruz, y tambien el de su
cuñado Gabriel Hdez. 614-19-81

(16)   293300   ext 6446 Cd. Juárez
(14)   293300   ext 4413 Chihuahua
(15)   616300   ext 7008 Cuauhtemoc
(13)   239300   ext 7250, 7261 Parral

Claudia, we were born in the same year. When you started working a forty-five-hour week, I was in high school cutting pictures of Kurt Cobain out of *Kerrang!* magazine, pasting them onto the cover of my agenda. I was in the washroom with an eyeliner pencil and a compact of powder trying to cover it all up. You were coming home so tired, maybe smelling like the exhaust from the bus that took you into and out of the maquiladora factory zone. Maybe you sat with your best friend, Idet, drinking coffee with condensed milk. Or maybe you made your favorite dinner, enchiladas with extra cheese. Maybe you sat twisting the laces of your blue Guess sneakers and dreaming of transformation.

Claudia, it's been four months, your life sitting in my closet. Am I any closer to knowing what it feels like to start assembling electrical cables from the age of fifteen? To kneel in front of a statue of the Virgin and promise to be pious? Me, with the blue eyes and the bagful of Barbies in my basement? Your life in my closet, Claudia. It hasn't felt right from the start.

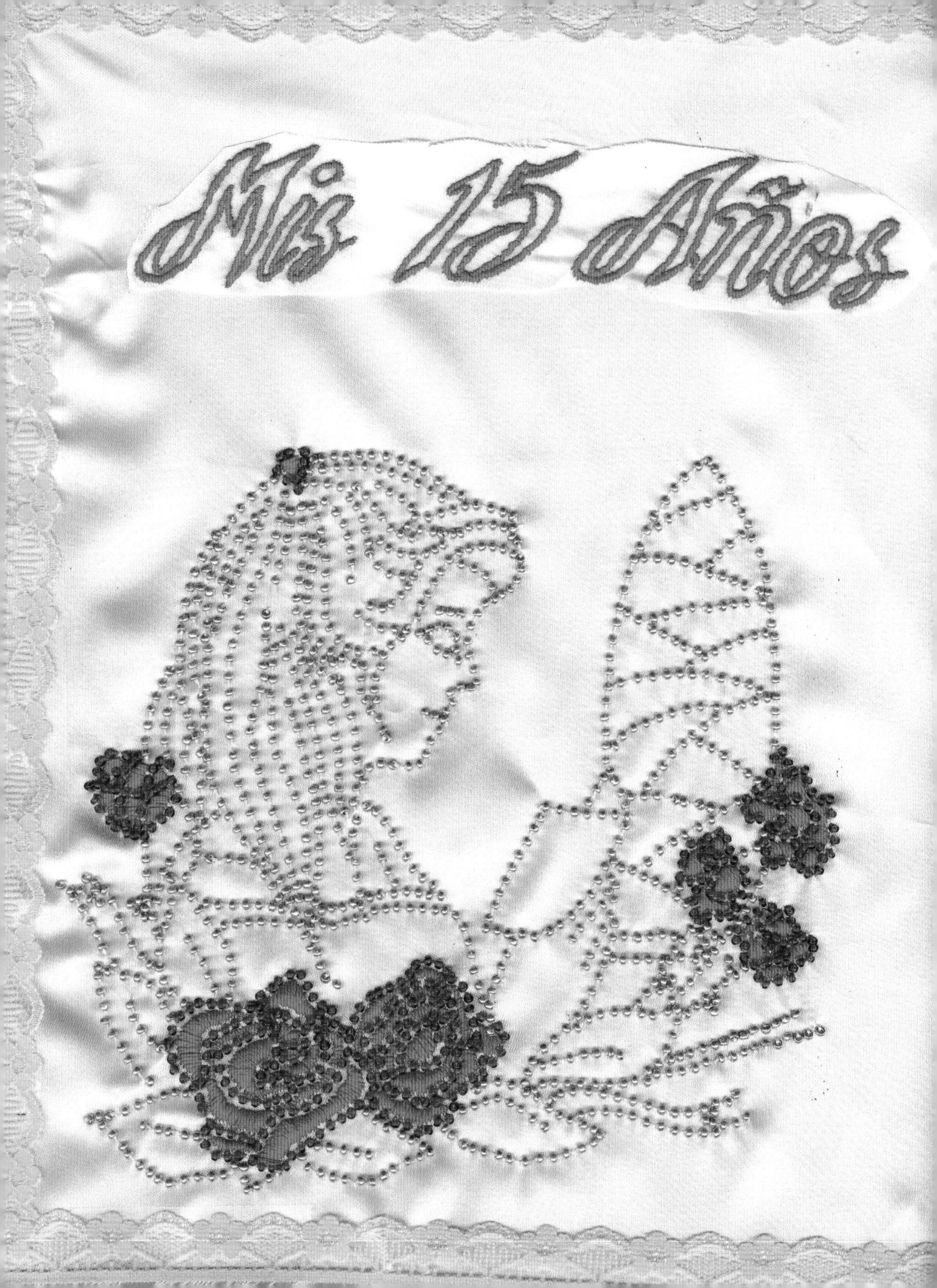
Mis 15 Años

La quinceñera, your fifteenth birthday, the day the world is pink and white, pearls and lace, the girl becomes the woman, the day she receives the body of Christ in communion. When a young lady celebrates her *quinceñera,* it is not only a celebration, but also a time to reflect. Usually, there will be a theme: Cinderella, bears, angels, dolls. The young lady will carry a bouquet of roses. The catering is traditional: mole, rice, chicken, tamales. To begin, the young lady will present her bouquet to the Virgin Mary. She will recite a poem that she has written herself. There will be a live deejay or a mariachi band. She will be given a last doll made from porcelain to represent the final offering of childhood. A carriage will take her to and from the reception. She must attend the beauty salon that day. Her hair must be arranged in rolls and knots, the silver-frosted flowers arranged with pins; her nails should match the pink of the dress. Then there is the jewelry. A ring symbolizes the commitment between the young lady and Christ. She will wear the metal charm of her patron saint. On her head must sit the crown, which represents the Crown of Life, promised in the Bible to faithful Christians. Gloves are optional, but pretty.

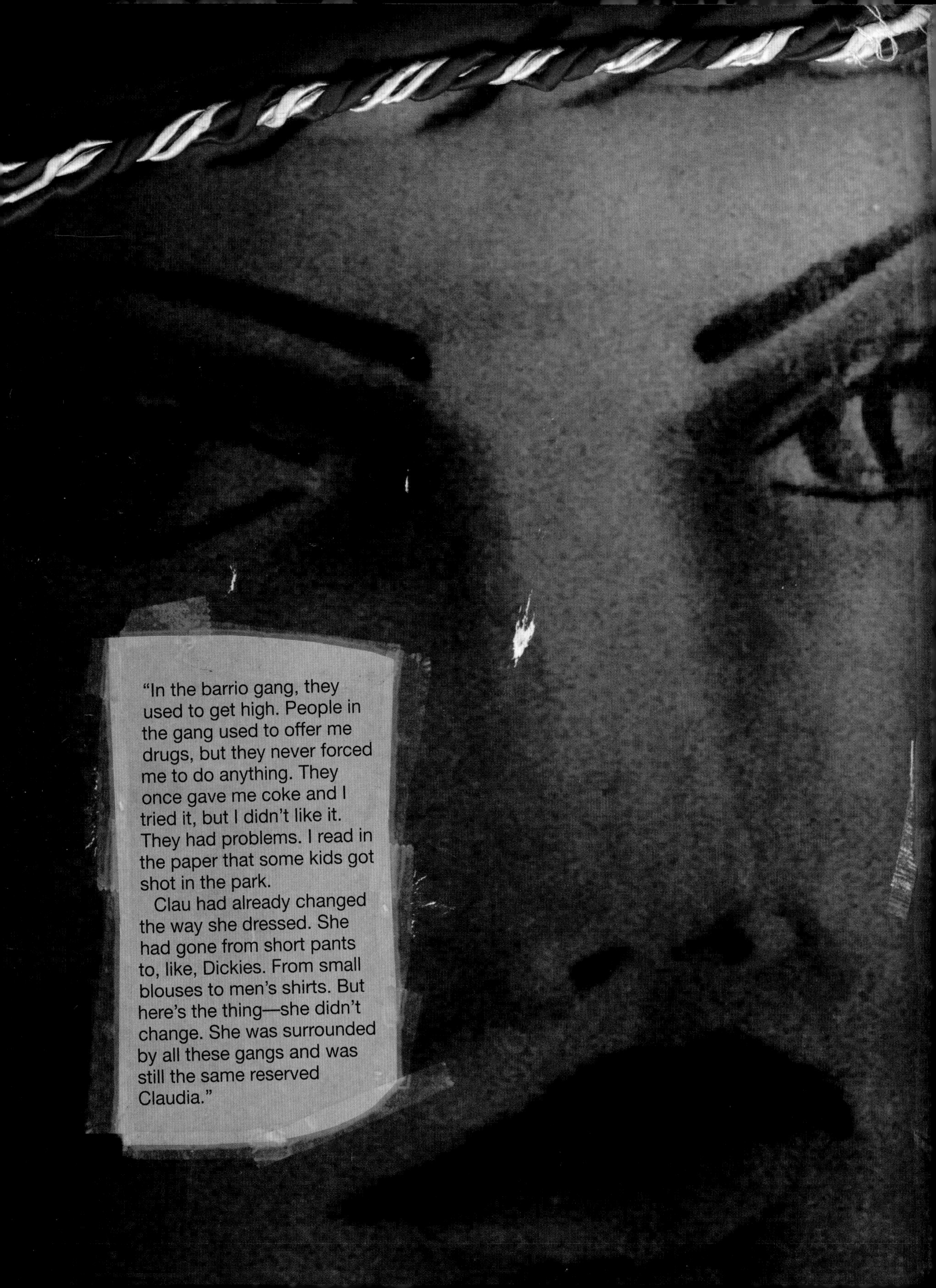

"In the barrio gang, they used to get high. People in the gang used to offer me drugs, but they never forced me to do anything. They once gave me coke and I tried it, but I didn't like it. They had problems. I read in the paper that some kids got shot in the park.

Clau had already changed the way she dressed. She had gone from short pants to, like, Dickies. From small blouses to men's shirts. But here's the thing—she didn't change. She was surrounded by all these gangs and was still the same reserved Claudia."

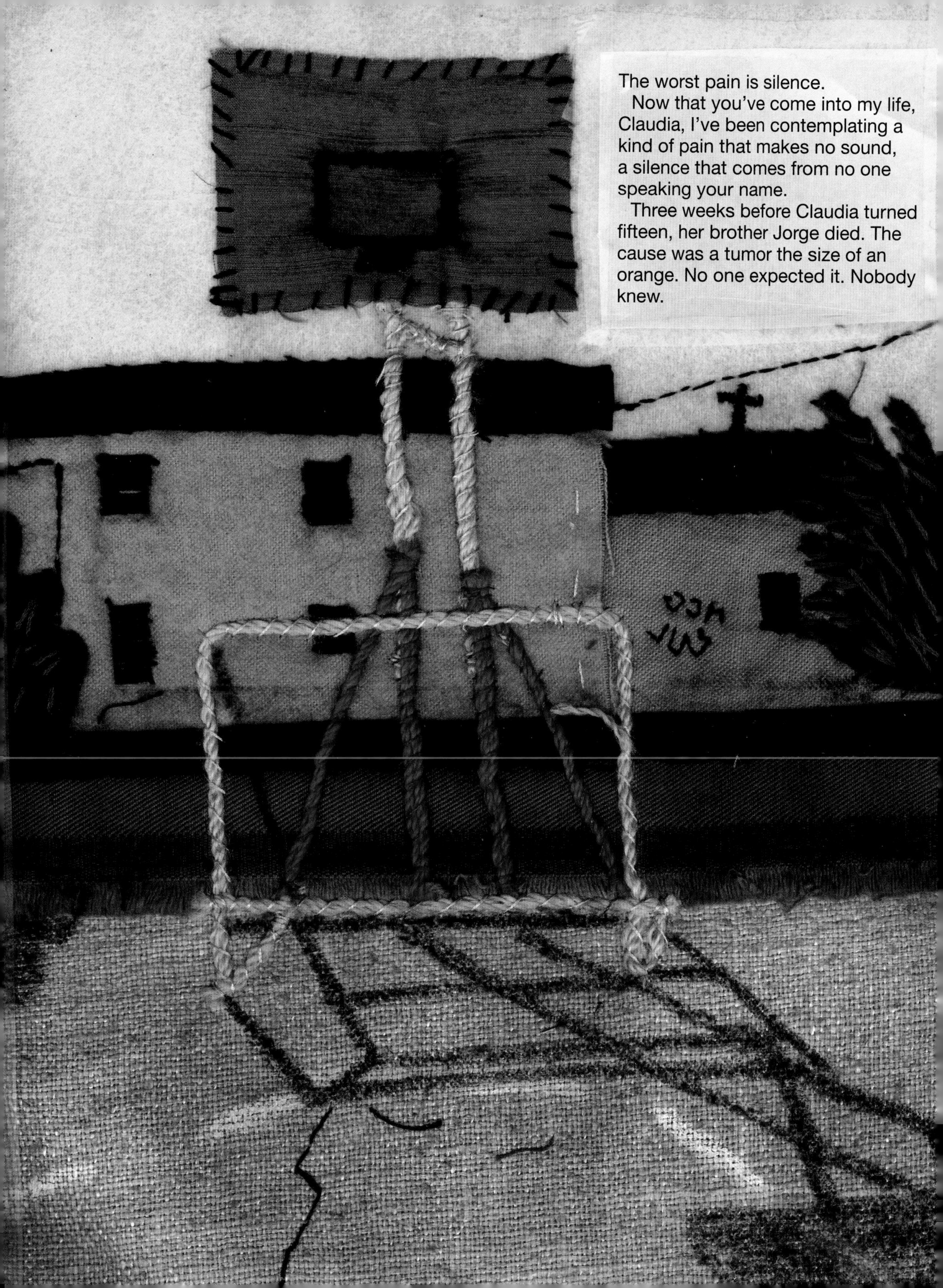

The worst pain is silence.

Now that you've come into my life, Claudia, I've been contemplating a kind of pain that makes no sound, a silence that comes from no one speaking your name.

Three weeks before Claudia turned fifteen, her brother Jorge died. The cause was a tumor the size of an orange. No one expected it. Nobody knew.

"When she turned fifteen we made her a small cake and she was happy. She wanted something bigger but her family didn't have the money. She started making plans to find a job. We altered her papers and she got what she wanted—a job in a factory."

Lear Corporation is a manufacturer of automotive interiors. Factory 173 is housed in three sprawling buildings in the maquiladora zone. Buses let the workers off two blocks from the entrance and everyone walks in their blue smocks or coveralls. At age fifteen, Claudia joined the procession. She would forget about Jorge in his inexpensive casket. She would forget her *quinceñera* because there was nothing to remember.

There is no sense in waiting for someone else to organize your party. If you want a beautiful life, you must work for it.

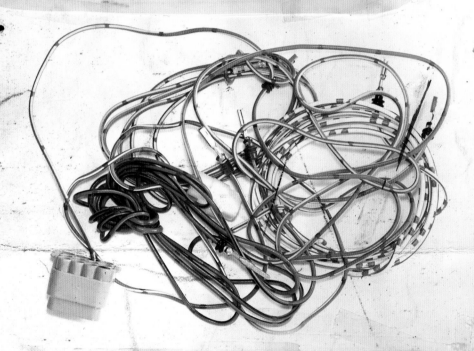

"To assemble the cable, you need connectors. There are sequences you need to follow to prevent any inverted circuits. For example, the sequence that we work with shows the color of the circuit, the connector it has to go to, and the connection point that completes the assembly. If it requires a red with a white, and instead I use a rose with a green, that circuit will be inverted, and that is a defect that will be rejected by the quality department. If we have two or three inverted circuits, we get a warning. If there are a few over a week, they can send us home for a day."

[redacted] CORPORATION

COMPANIA: Lagr Electrical Systems de Mexico S de R. L. de C.V

IMSS: 33035772107
RFC.: LES360315DN7
INFONAVIT: 080034918

00786

FOLIO: 00785

NUMERO	NOMBRE	RFC.	REG. DEL IMSS	PLANTA
602190	GONZALEZ CLAUDIA IVETH	COCL510205::5	35728147877	273

FECHA INGRESO	SUELDO DARIO	FECHA PAGO	PERIODO DE PAGO DEL	AL	DEPARTAMENTO CELULA	TURNO	AREA	CUENTA
02/12/1998	67.92	01/14/2001	01/08/2001	01/14/2001	712	2	5	5001

PERCEPCIONES	HORAS/DIAS	IMPORTE	DEDUCCIONES	IMPORTE	SALDO
Sueldo normal	44.24	467.41	IMSP	22.24	
Bono Asist Semanal D		64.52	Desc. por Alimentos	40.15	
Bono de Antiguedad D		47.03	Cuota Sindical	0.50	
S normal Adeudo Gra	18	190.18	Fondo de Ahorro	55.76	559.30
Credito al Salario		15.28			

TOTAL PERCEPTIONAS 784.42
TOTAL DEDUCCIONES 128.85

DEPOSITO EN BANCO
CUENTA BANCARIA

TOTAL CUPONES 202.00

NETO EFECTIVO 555.57

LUNES		MARTES		MIERCOLES		JUEVES		VIERNES		SABADO		DOMINGO	
8.87	Tiempo Re	8.80	Tiempo Reg	8.87	Tiempo Reg	8.87	Tiempo Re	8.53	Tiempo Reg	18.00	Tiempo Reg		

RECISI DE CONFORMIDAD LA CANTIDAD ANOTADA EN ESTE RECISO POR LOS CONCEPTOS EN EL ESPECIFICADOS CON LO CUAL ME HAN SIDO PAGADOS POR LA EMPRESA TODAS LOS SALARIOS Y PRESTATIONES LEGALES Y CONTRACTUALES A QUE PUCIERA TENER DERECHO.

FIRMA EMPLEADO

**La confianza es la pieza mas importante para el exito of proyecto

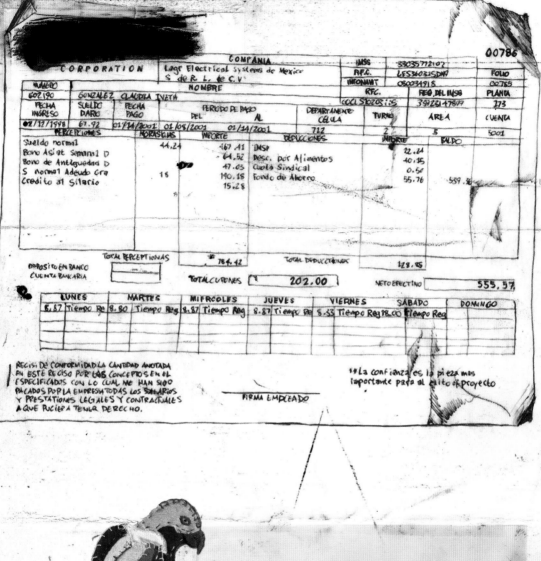

Q: "And what do you think about on the assembly line?"

A: "Well, you cannot go thinking about anything. You have to be 99 percent concentrated on your work to prevent any defects."

The cotton field that is not a cotton field: The imagination goes to work, looking at this empty place. You want the blankness to yield answers, to communicate a story. But no. The field is a kind of nowhere, a clearinghouse of objects left behind and unwanted. There is no possession here, only supervision. A stern sun overhead. A police car at the edge of the cracked earth, idling.

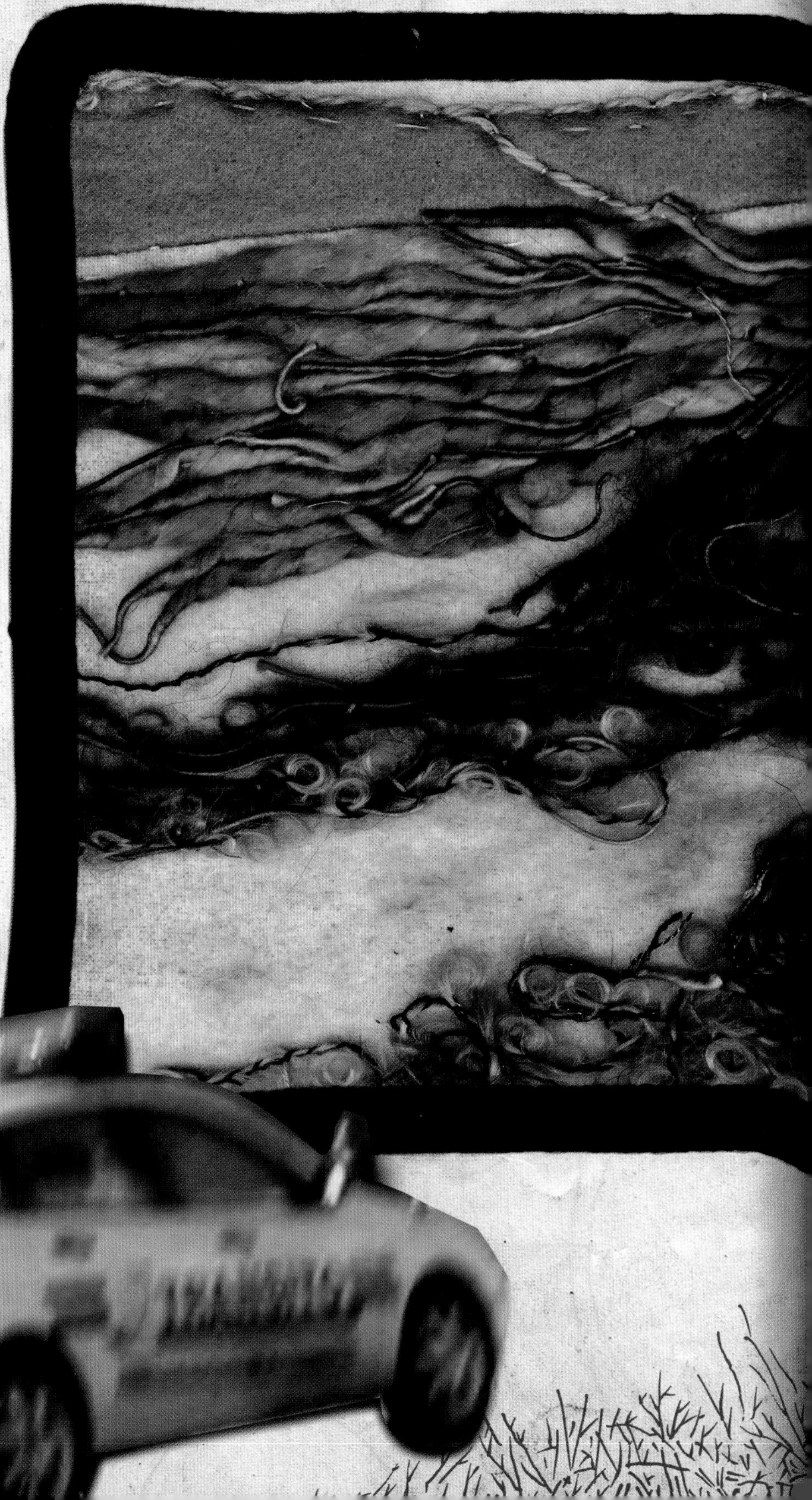

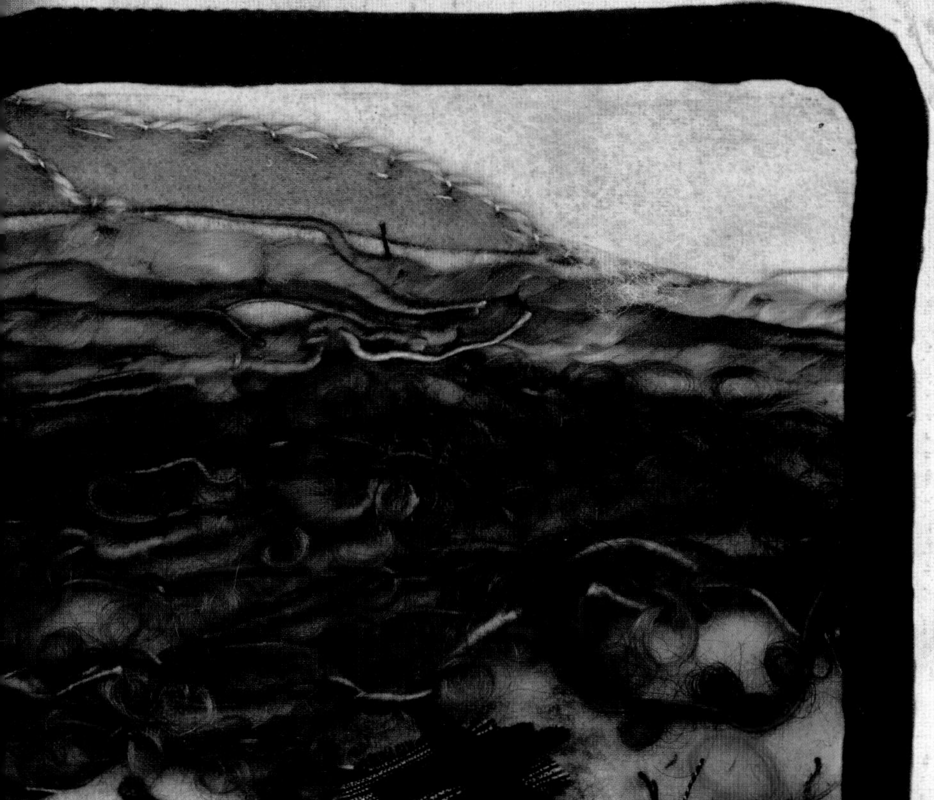

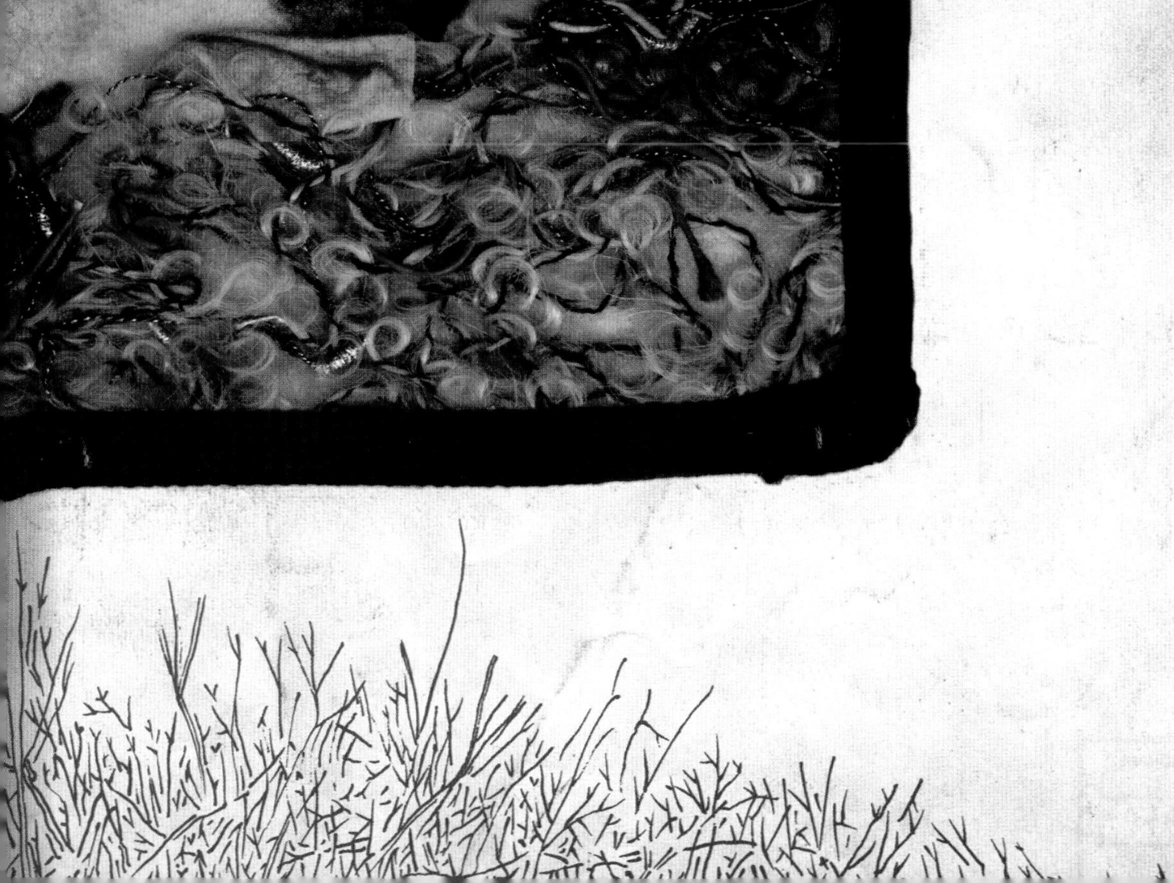

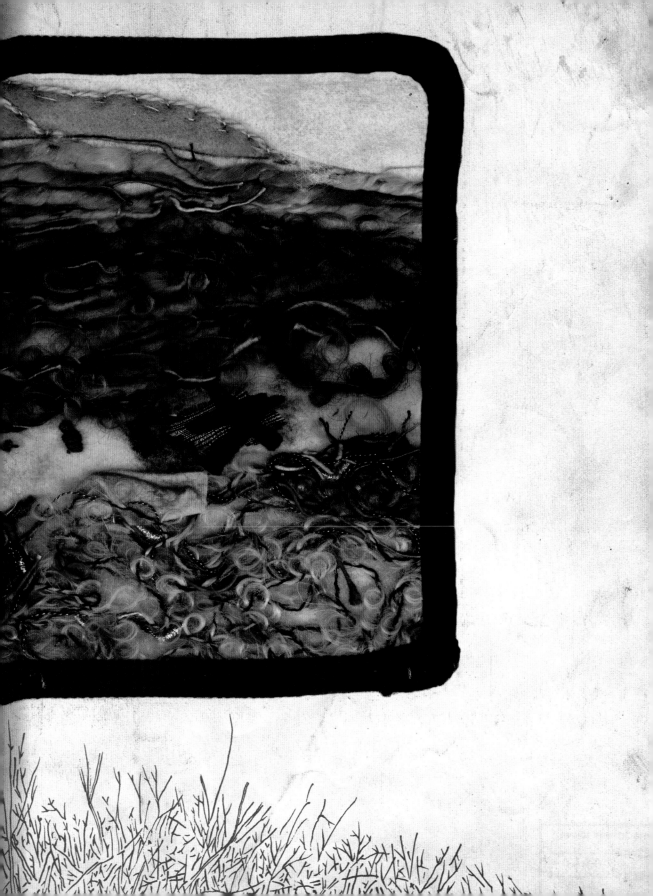

"And then she met Victor. She met him on the assembly line at Lear. He told her that he liked her and asked her to go to the movies. And then she fell in love. And it was the first time. They would spend Sundays together.

And one day she asks me if she is walking funny. And I said no, and then she told me she had lost her virginity to Victor."

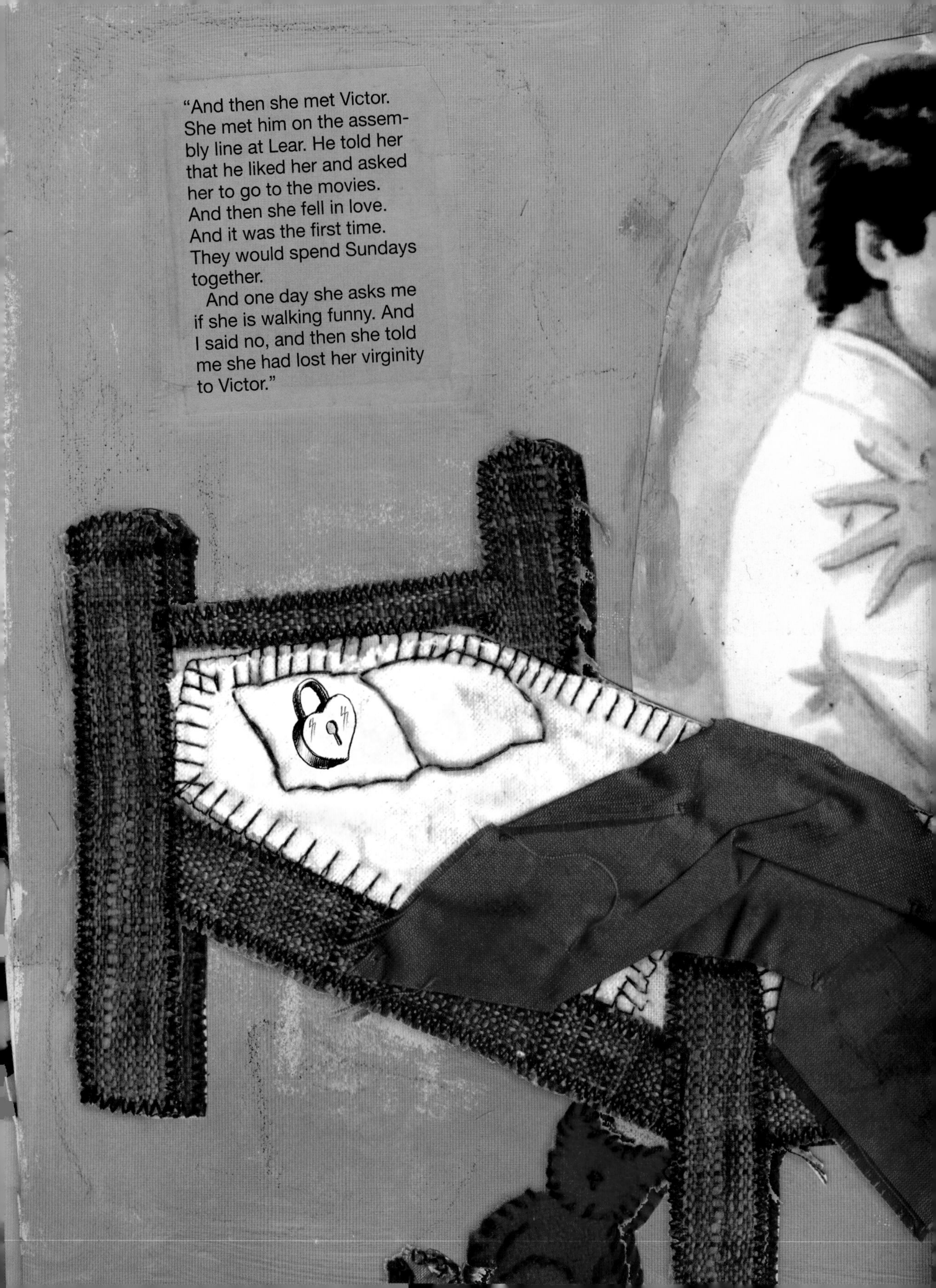

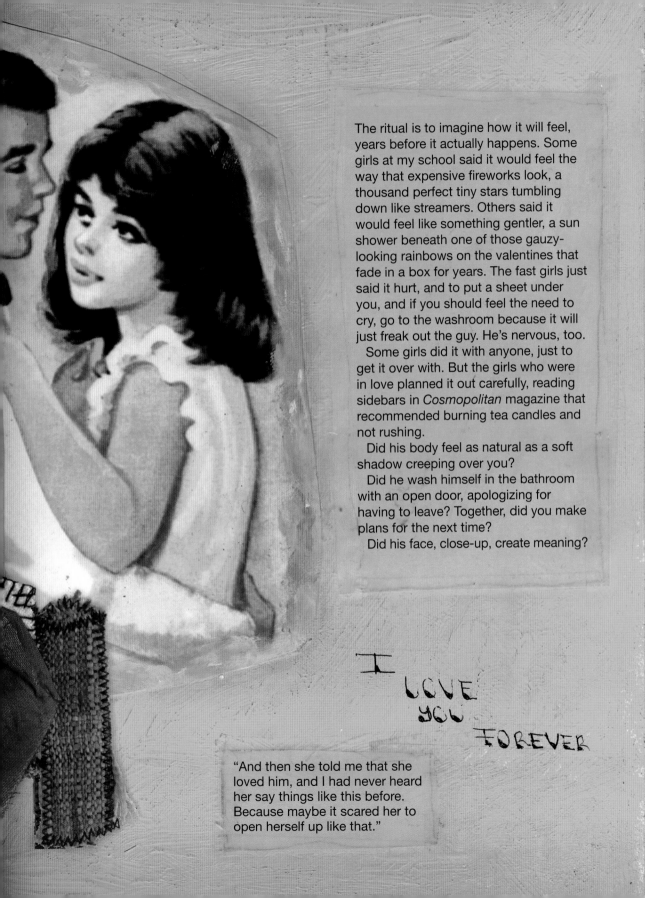

The ritual is to imagine how it will feel, years before it actually happens. Some girls at my school said it would feel the way that expensive fireworks look, a thousand perfect tiny stars tumbling down like streamers. Others said it would feel like something gentler, a sun shower beneath one of those gauzy-looking rainbows on the valentines that fade in a box for years. The fast girls just said it hurt, and to put a sheet under you, and if you should feel the need to cry, go to the washroom because it will just freak out the guy. He's nervous, too.

Some girls did it with anyone, just to get it over with. But the girls who were in love planned it out carefully, reading sidebars in *Cosmopolitan* magazine that recommended burning tea candles and not rushing.

Did his body feel as natural as a soft shadow creeping over you?

Did he wash himself in the bathroom with an open door, apologizing for having to leave? Together, did you make plans for the next time?

Did his face, close-up, create meaning?

I LOVE YOU FOREVER

"And then she told me that she loved him, and I had never heard her say things like this before. Because maybe it scared her to open herself up like that."

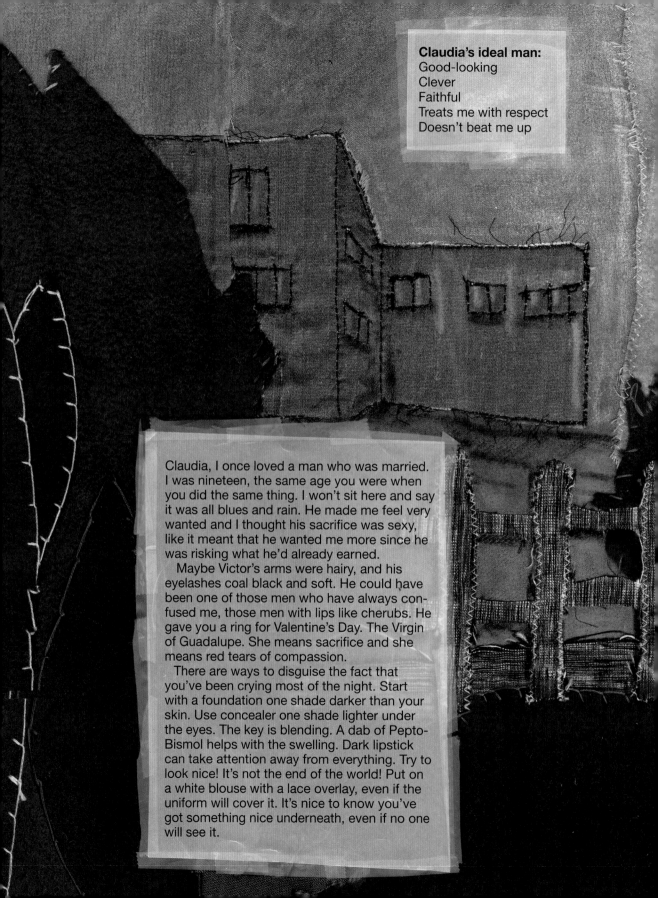

Claudia's ideal man:
Good-looking
Clever
Faithful
Treats me with respect
Doesn't beat me up

Claudia, I once loved a man who was married.
I was nineteen, the same age you were when
you did the same thing. I won't sit here and say
it was all blues and rain. He made me feel very
wanted and I thought his sacrifice was sexy,
like it meant that he wanted me more since he
was risking what he'd already earned.

Maybe Victor's arms were hairy, and his
eyelashes coal black and soft. He could have
been one of those men who have always con-
fused me, those men with lips like cherubs. He
gave you a ring for Valentine's Day. The Virgin
of Guadalupe. She means sacrifice and she
means red tears of compassion.

There are ways to disguise the fact that
you've been crying most of the night. Start
with a foundation one shade darker than your
skin. Use concealer one shade lighter under
the eyes. The key is blending. A dab of Pepto-
Bismol helps with the swelling. Dark lipstick
can take attention away from everything. Try to
look nice! It's not the end of the world! Put on
a white blouse with a lace overlay, even if the
uniform will cover it. It's nice to know you've
got something nice underneath, even if no one
will see it.

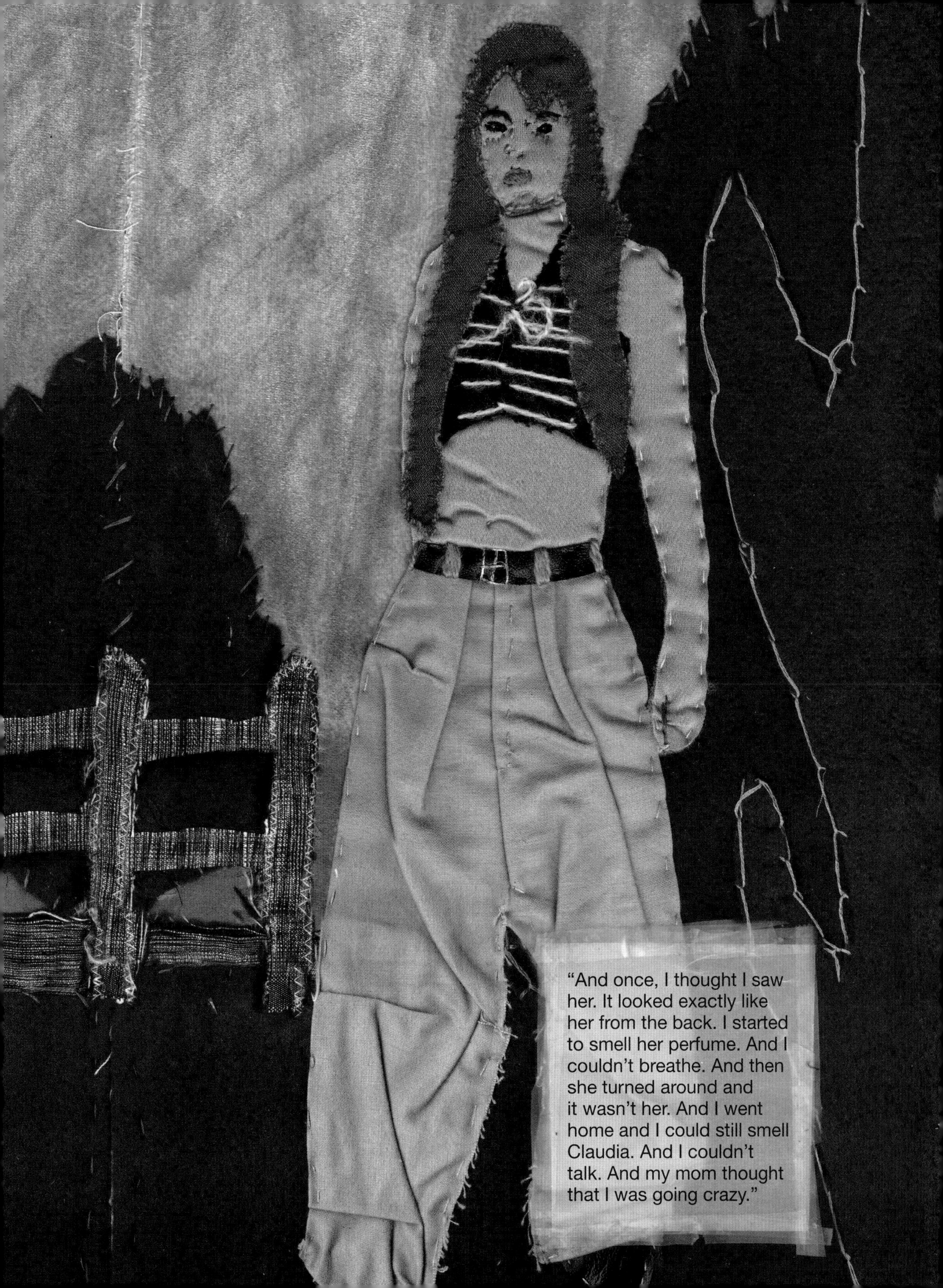
"And once, I thought I saw her. It looked exactly like her from the back. I started to smell her perfume. And I couldn't breathe. And then she turned around and it wasn't her. And I went home and I could still smell Claudia. And I couldn't talk. And my mom thought that I was going crazy."

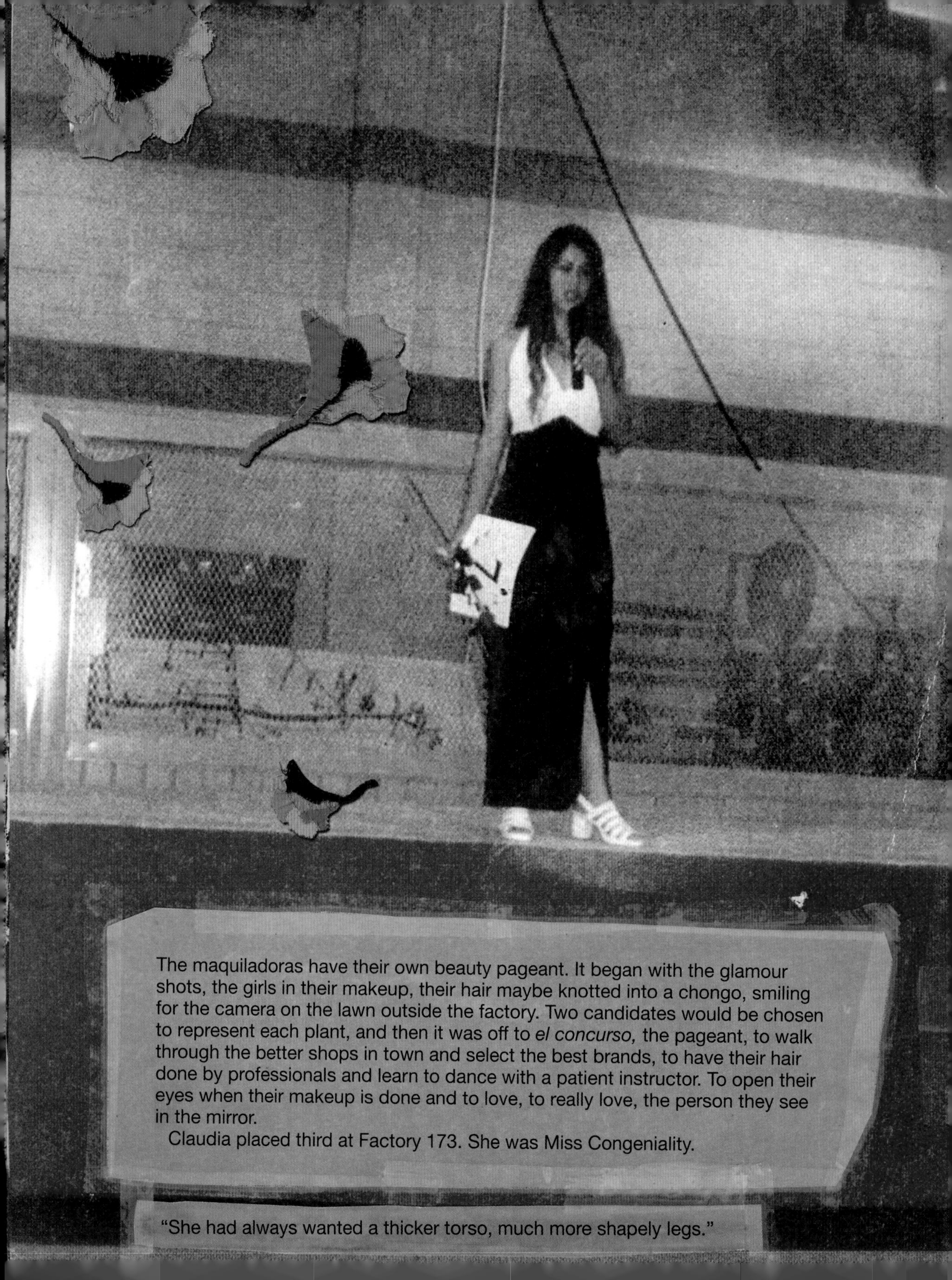

The maquiladoras have their own beauty pageant. It began with the glamour shots, the girls in their makeup, their hair maybe knotted into a chongo, smiling for the camera on the lawn outside the factory. Two candidates would be chosen to represent each plant, and then it was off to *el concurso,* the pageant, to walk through the better shops in town and select the best brands, to have their hair done by professionals and learn to dance with a patient instructor. To open their eyes when their makeup is done and to love, to really love, the person they see in the mirror.

Claudia placed third at Factory 173. She was Miss Congeniality.

"She had always wanted a thicker torso, much more shapely legs."

A twenty-five-kilogram FedEx box. It arrived at my house four months ago. I needed to tell your story somehow, knowing that maybe this was none of my business. So before I cut the box open, I promised you my cuts would be soft. I was trying to cut you free.

Claudia, I'm ashamed to say that many of the promises I've made I have broken.

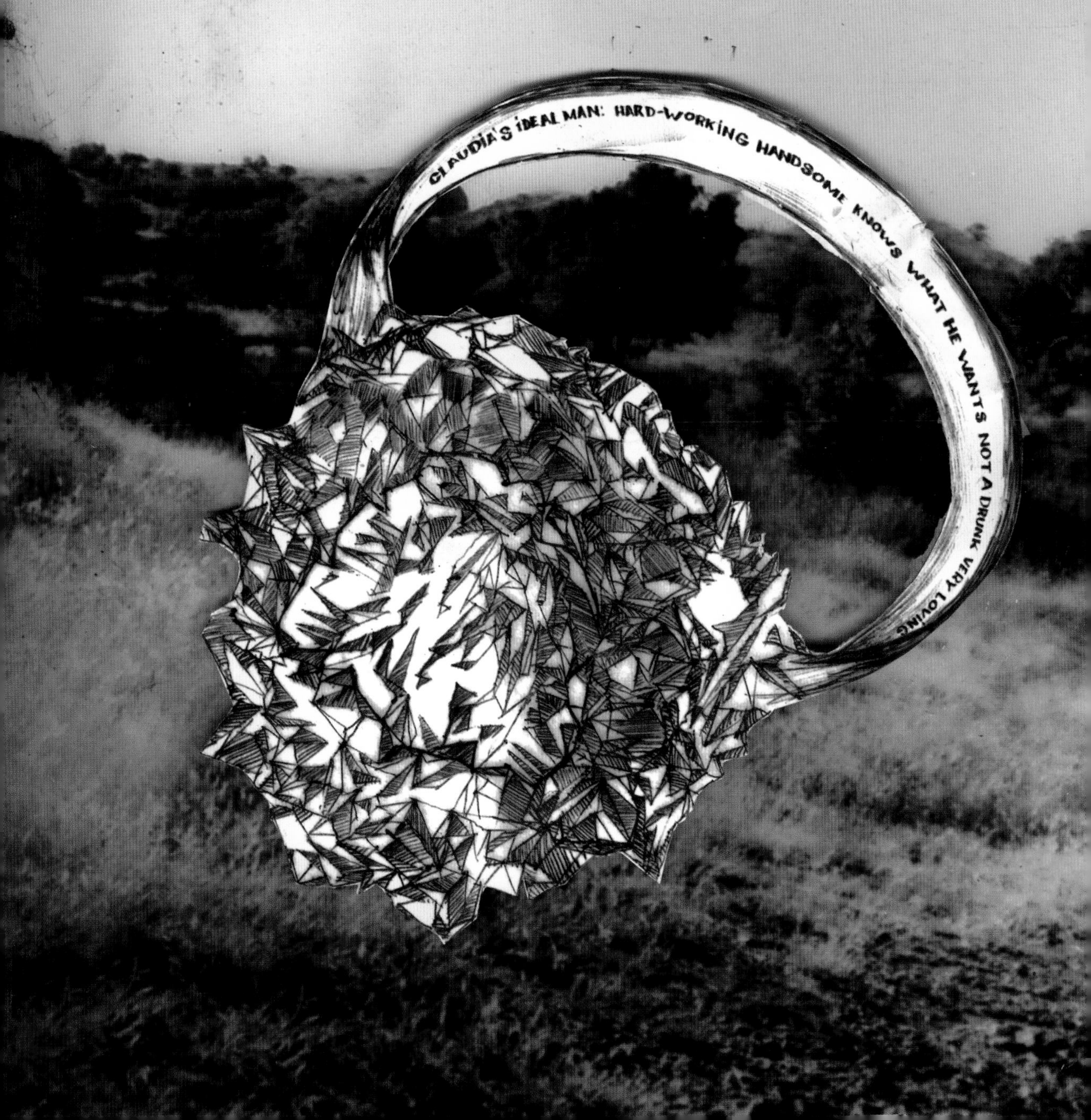
CLAUDIA'S IDEAL MAN: HARD-WORKING HANDSOME KNOWS WHAT HE WANTS NOT A DRUNK VERY LOVING

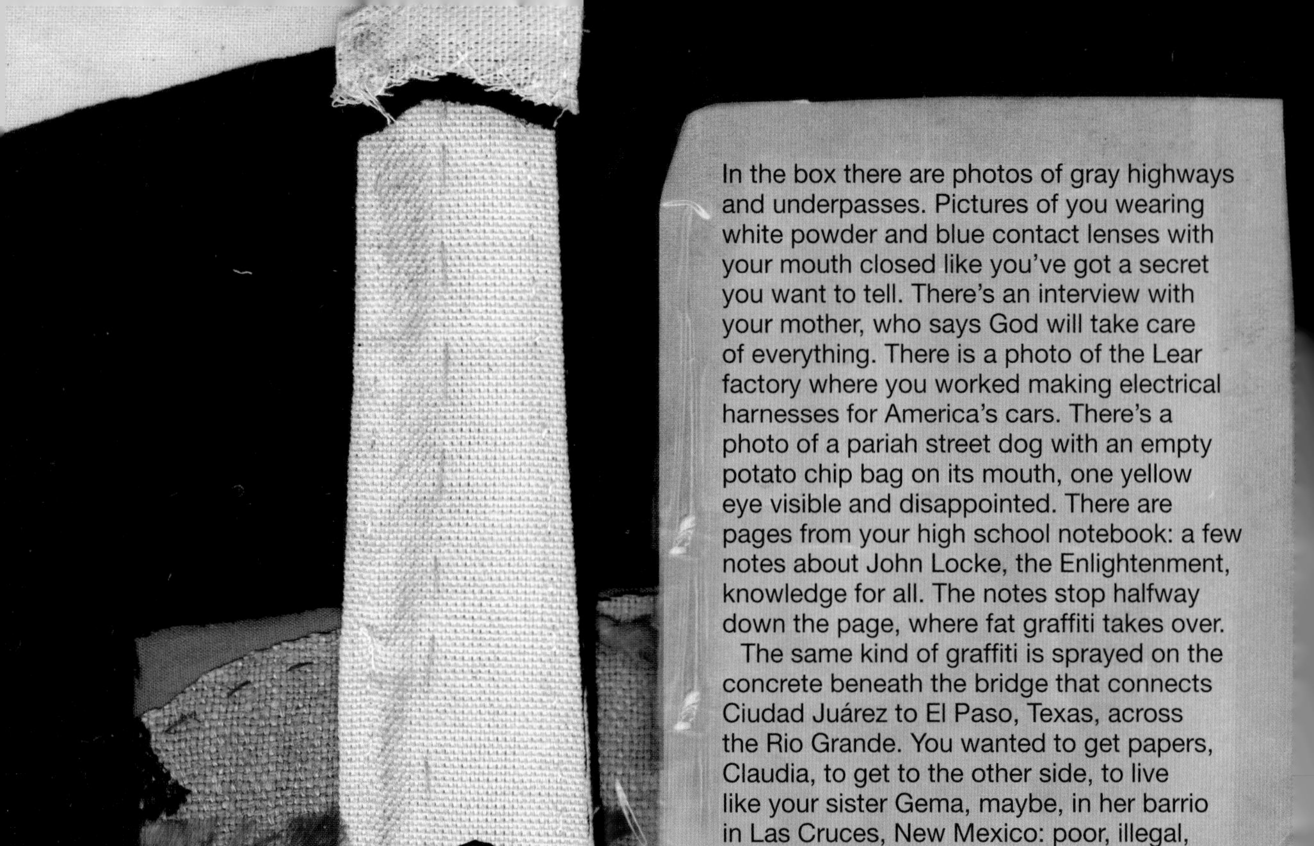

In the box there are photos of gray highways and underpasses. Pictures of you wearing white powder and blue contact lenses with your mouth closed like you've got a secret you want to tell. There's an interview with your mother, who says God will take care of everything. There is a photo of the Lear factory where you worked making electrical harnesses for America's cars. There's a photo of a pariah street dog with an empty potato chip bag on its mouth, one yellow eye visible and disappointed. There are pages from your high school notebook: a few notes about John Locke, the Enlightenment, knowledge for all. The notes stop halfway down the page, where fat graffiti takes over.

The same kind of graffiti is sprayed on the concrete beneath the bridge that connects Ciudad Juárez to El Paso, Texas, across the Rio Grande. You wanted to get papers, Claudia, to get to the other side, to live like your sister Gema, maybe, in her barrio in Las Cruces, New Mexico: poor, illegal, surrounded by gangs, with a boyfriend who writes to her from prison. Unable to cross into Mexico even to touch her mother's hands, even for a funeral. Gema, living in America, and somehow it all still is worth it.

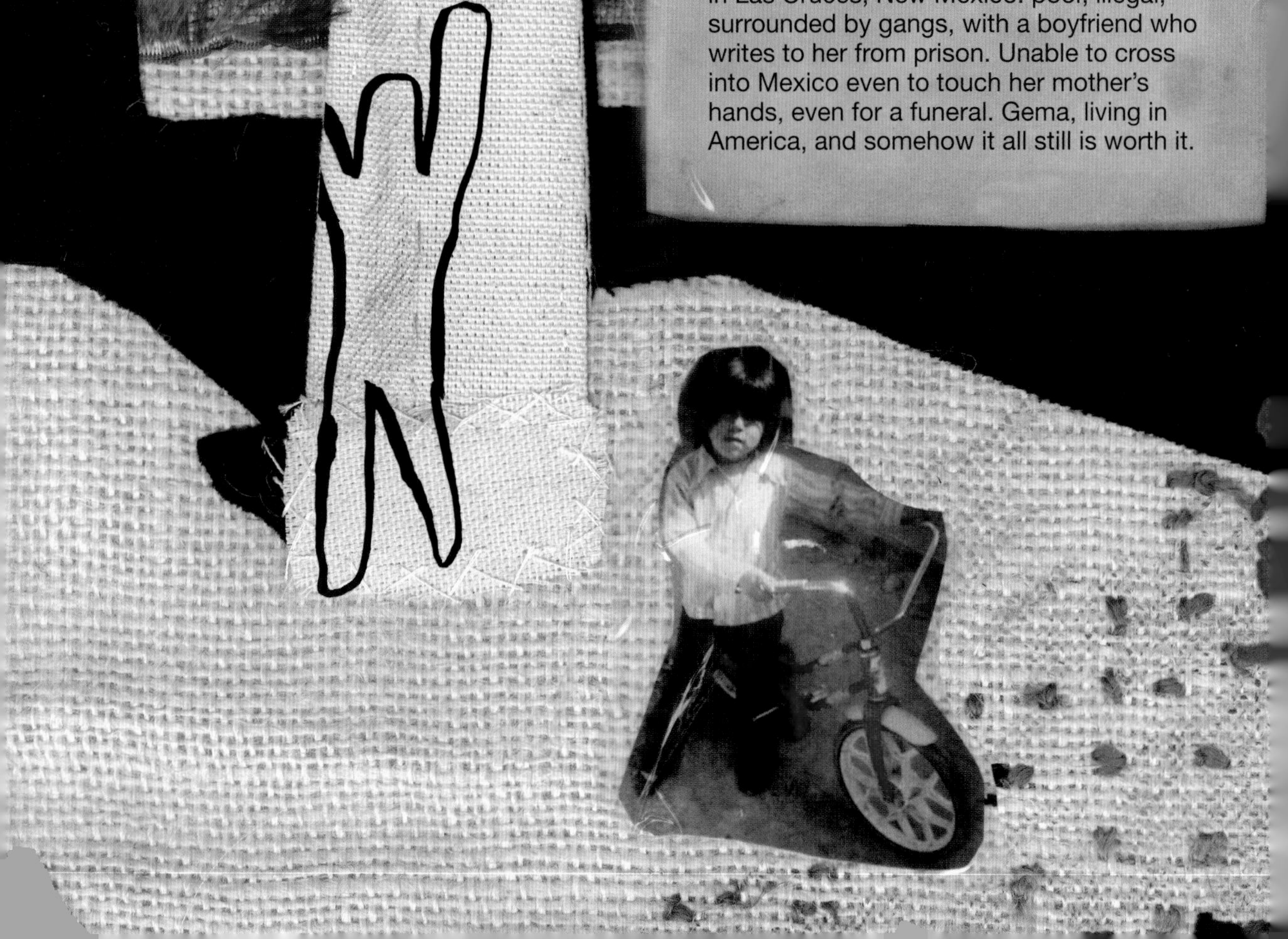

"She is quiet. Kind of weird. People would ask me, why do you hang out with such a weird person? But she is my best friend. She didn't like to talk that much. She didn't like to be hugged or touched.

I never learned how to roll. She would roll the joint. Sometimes we would get the munchies. Like, it was always thirty minutes after we smoked weed. Sometimes we would go to the *panadería.* We used to eat bread and make, like, milk shakes with bananas. Hot Cheetos. She really loved Hot Cheetos."

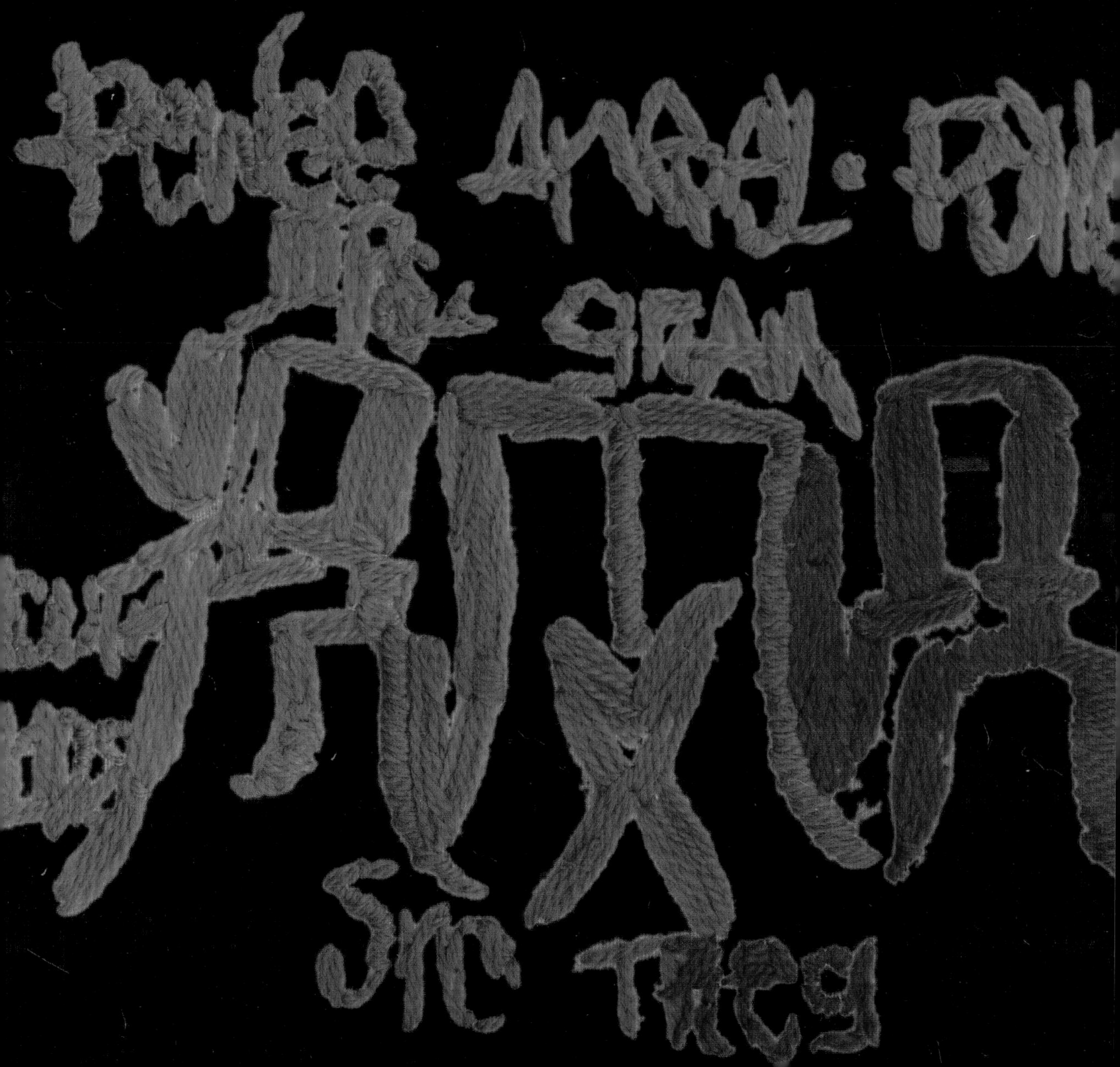

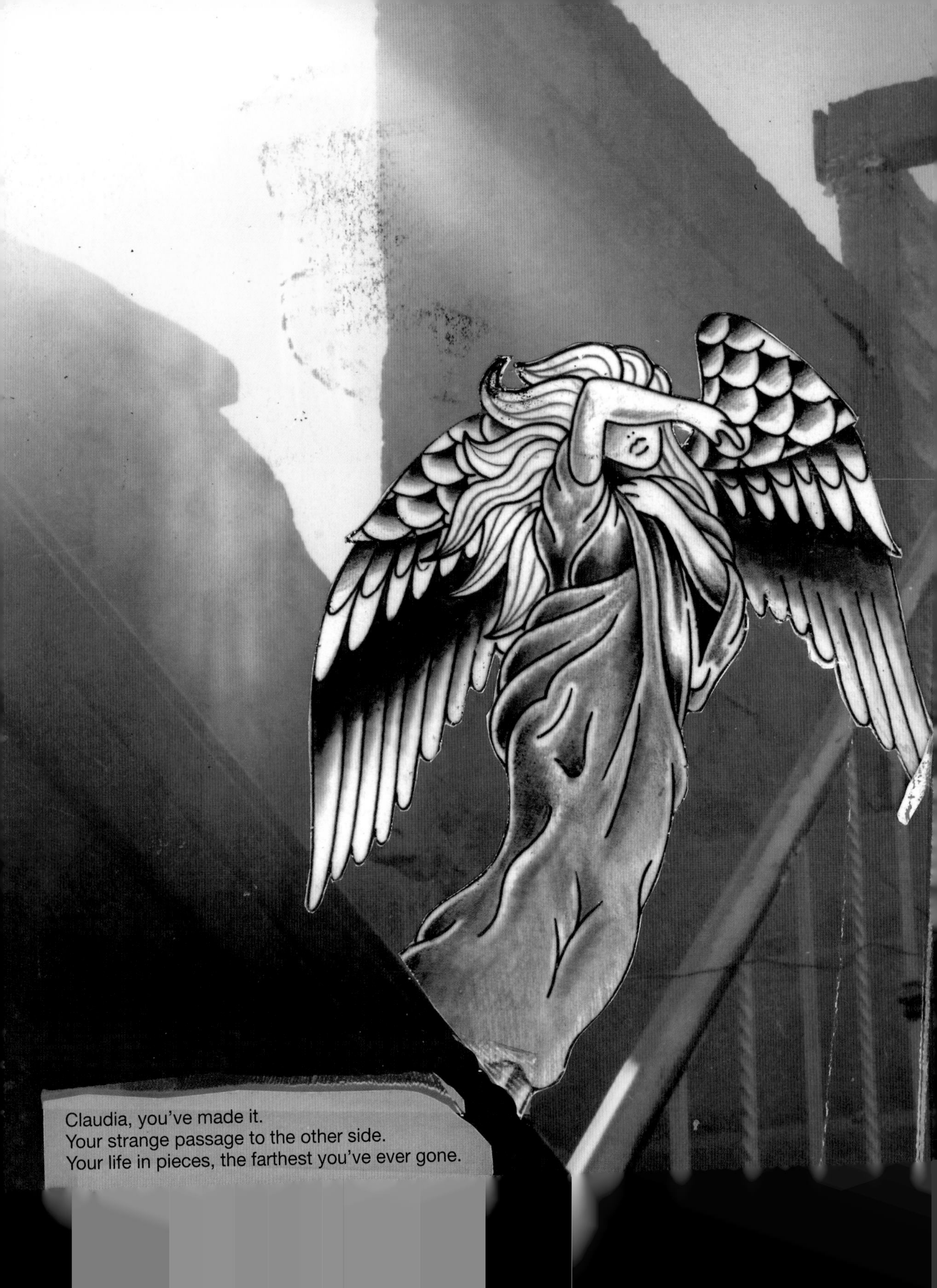
Claudia, you've made it.
Your strange passage to the other side.
Your life in pieces, the farthest you've ever gone.

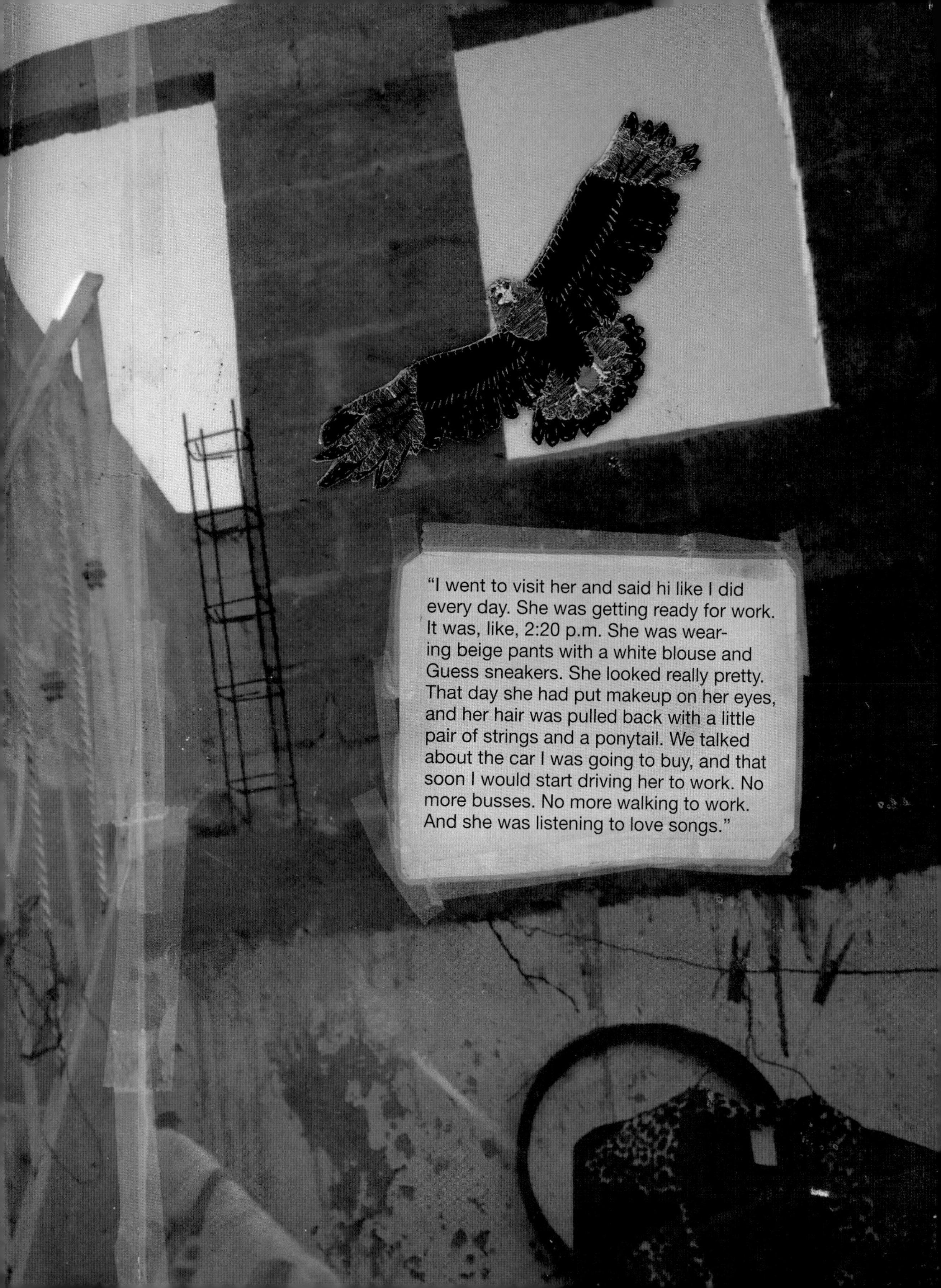
"I went to visit her and said hi like I did every day. She was getting ready for work. It was, like, 2:20 p.m. She was wearing beige pants with a white blouse and Guess sneakers. She looked really pretty. That day she had put makeup on her eyes, and her hair was pulled back with a little pair of strings and a ponytail. We talked about the car I was going to buy, and that soon I would start driving her to work. No more busses. No more walking to work. And she was listening to love songs."

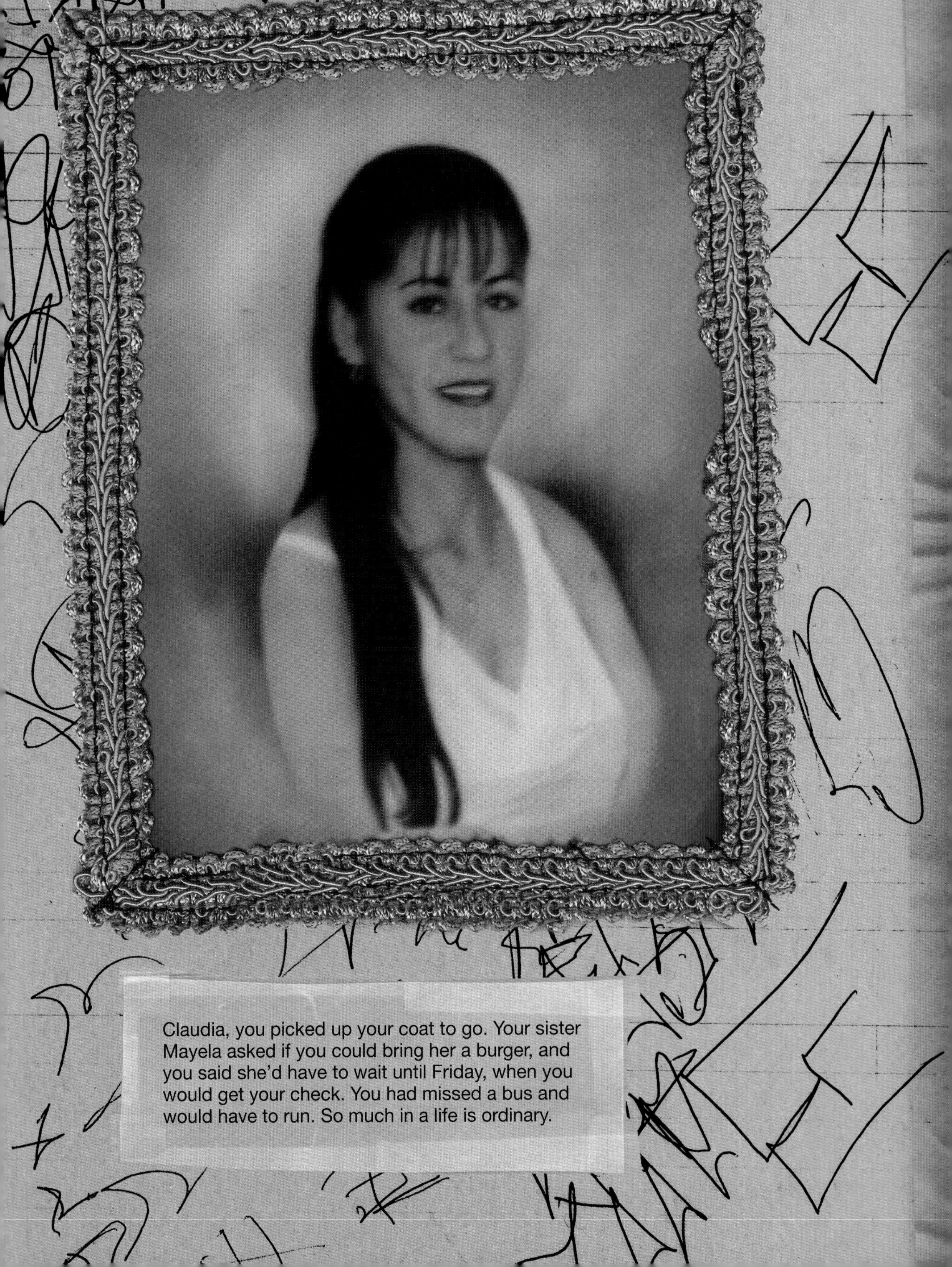

Claudia, you picked up your coat to go. Your sister Mayela asked if you could bring her a burger, and you said she'd have to wait until Friday, when you would get your check. You had missed a bus and would have to run. So much in a life is ordinary.

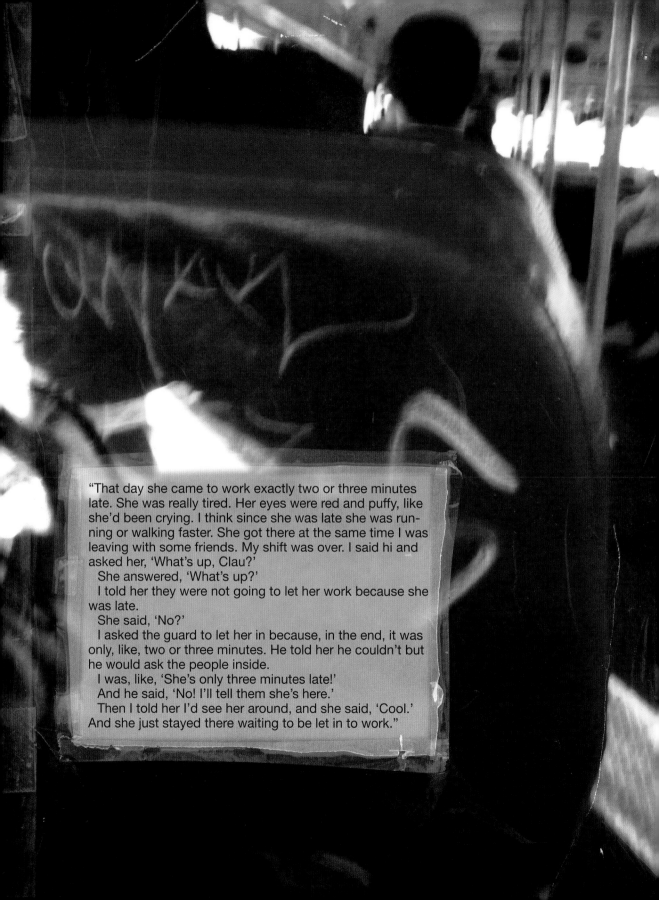

"That day she came to work exactly two or three minutes late. She was really tired. Her eyes were red and puffy, like she'd been crying. I think since she was late she was running or walking faster. She got there at the same time I was leaving with some friends. My shift was over. I said hi and asked her, 'What's up, Clau?'

She answered, 'What's up?'

I told her they were not going to let her work because she was late.

She said, 'No?'

I asked the guard to let her in because, in the end, it was only, like, two or three minutes. He told her he couldn't but he would ask the people inside.

I was, like, 'She's only three minutes late!'

And he said, 'No! I'll tell them she's here.'

Then I told her I'd see her around, and she said, 'Cool.' And she just stayed there waiting to be let in to work."

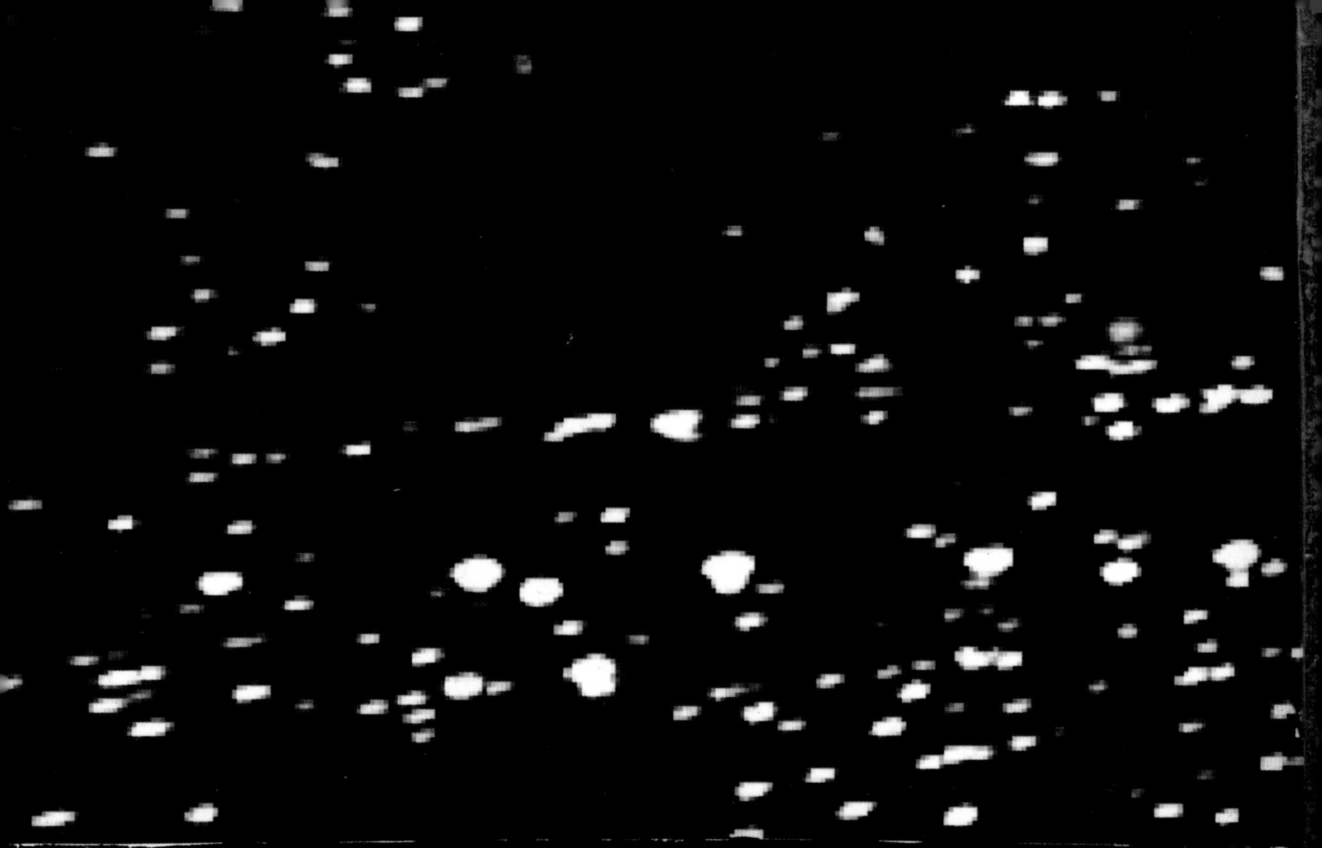

Idet stayed up all night for you, Claudia. Your best friend. Maybe she was thinking of the time when you were seven years old and you and Gema slipped away from your grandfather and disappeared. Gema, who now lives across the border in New Mexico. That time, the police brought you back, two scared, hungry, sunstruck kids.

A person vanishes from sight and all that remains are memories. Your sister Mayela remembers the secretive ways you showed affection. How you hugged and kissed her daughters only if you thought that no one was looking, how her daughter Carla could always fall asleep if you were in the bed beside her. Your sudden disappearance reminded Mayela how strong you were. How you could keep everything bottled up inside.

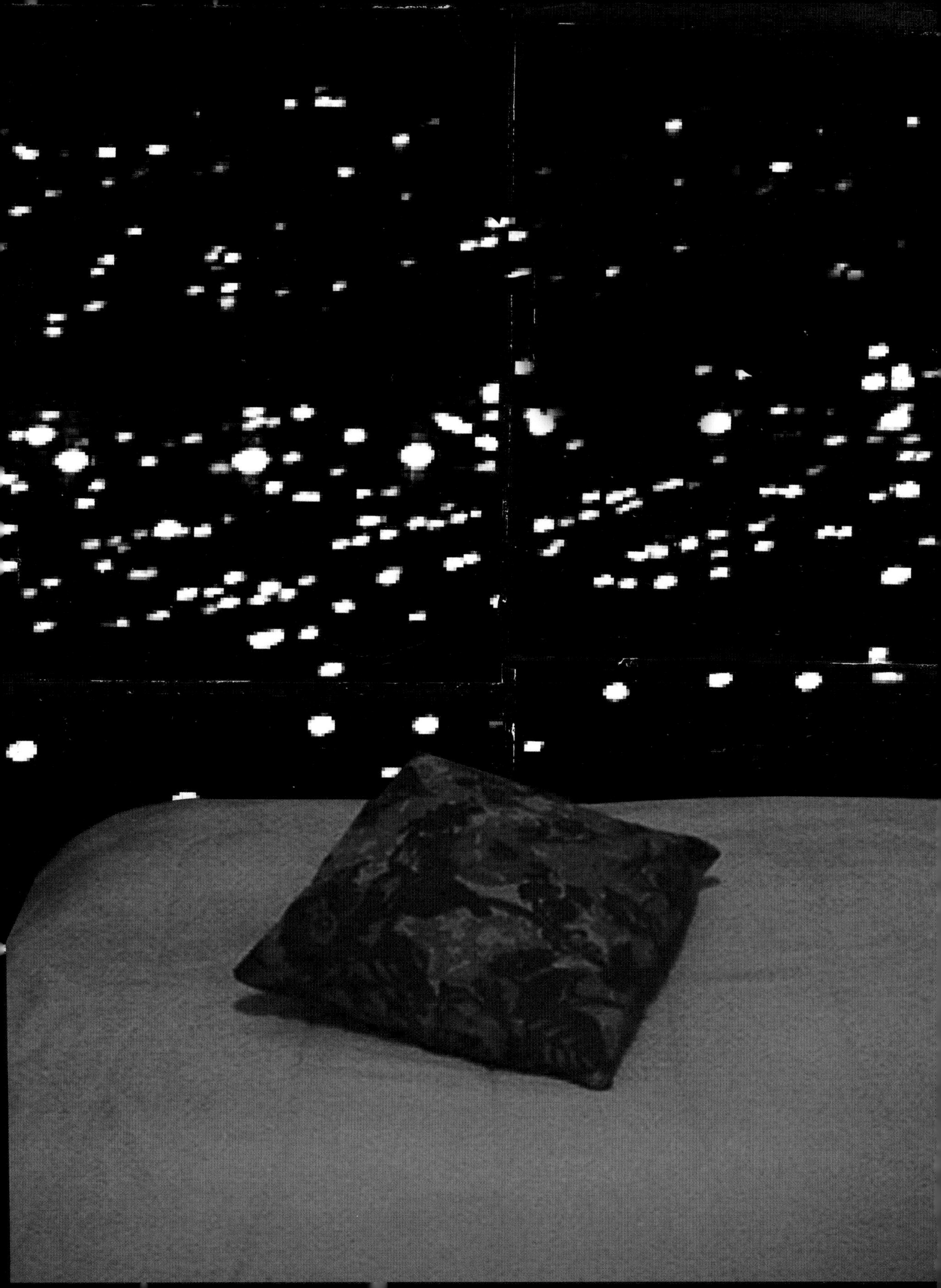

SUPERPOSICION OSEO-FACIAL

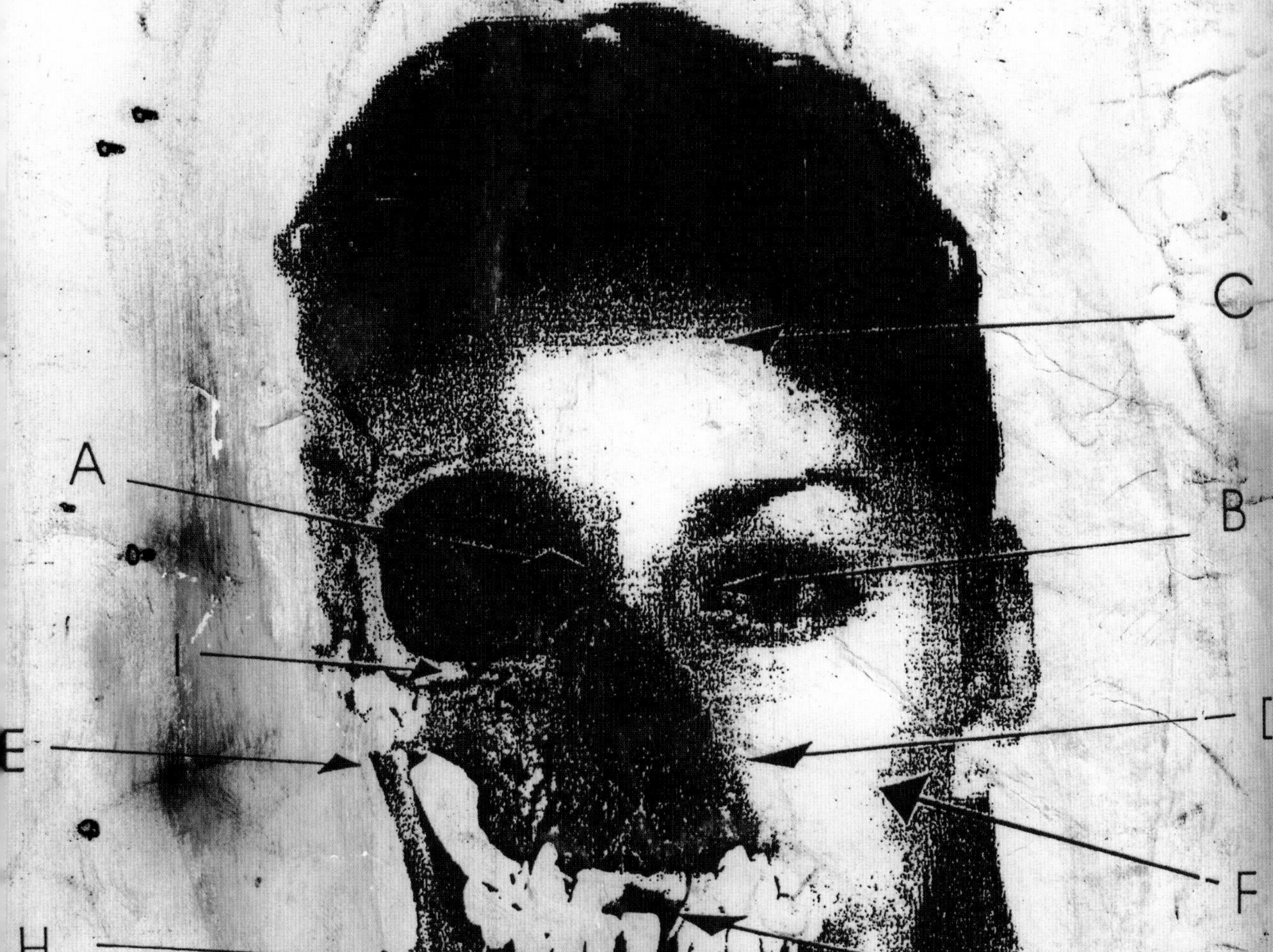
A
B
C
D
E
F
G
H
I
J

FEMENINA NO IDENTIFICADA 189/01
CLAUDIA IVETTE GONZALEZ

proximada de ciento cincuenta metros en direccion ori

e la Avenida Ejercito Nacional y Cuatrocientos metro

a Avenida Paseo de la Victoria, y tomando como punt

eferencia un puente de concreto que se encuentra,

“At the solicitor’s office, they said that they couldn’t process a missing person’s report. She had to be missing for seventy-two hours.

On Friday, October 12, the missing-person’s report was made. I didn’t understand the questions the police were asking. They wanted to know if she was a drug addict, asking if maybe she ran away with her boyfriend. Then they asked if she was really open and slutty with guys.”

irve al ... e irrigación

redio al ... donde se d

rejudic ... a vista debajo del puente en mer

una distancia aproximada de ochenta centímetros

ene a la vista **UN CADAVER** del sexo femenino, el

resenta signos de muerte real y no reciente, su estad

onservación es incompleta, encontrándose en

osición de decúbito dorsal, con su extremidad cefalic

irección al oriente, sus extremidades inferiores

irección opuestas y flexionadas, mientras que

xtremidades superiores se encuentras unidas entre si

n cordón de ... vueltas en

nuñeca, dic ... su totalidad

a región ab ... de que

xtremidades se encuentran bajo la region lumbar,

The night before, you were crying in your room—crying over Victor. You closed the door to your room, and you cried. Did your body feel like an unsafe house, some terrible containment? Did the crying feel like thunder drumming the walls of your chest? Curled up, maybe you felt a little bit protected. A bean in its dark place. I imagine that you lay in the nest of your bed, curled inside your favorite jacket, the Dallas Cowboys one with the iron-on blue satin star. The music was very loud. Without Victor your body felt uncomfortable, less useful, a sealed and trembling jar.

adáver es de la siguiente media filiación: es

omplexión regular, de tez morena, con una est

proximada de un metro con sesenta y tres cen

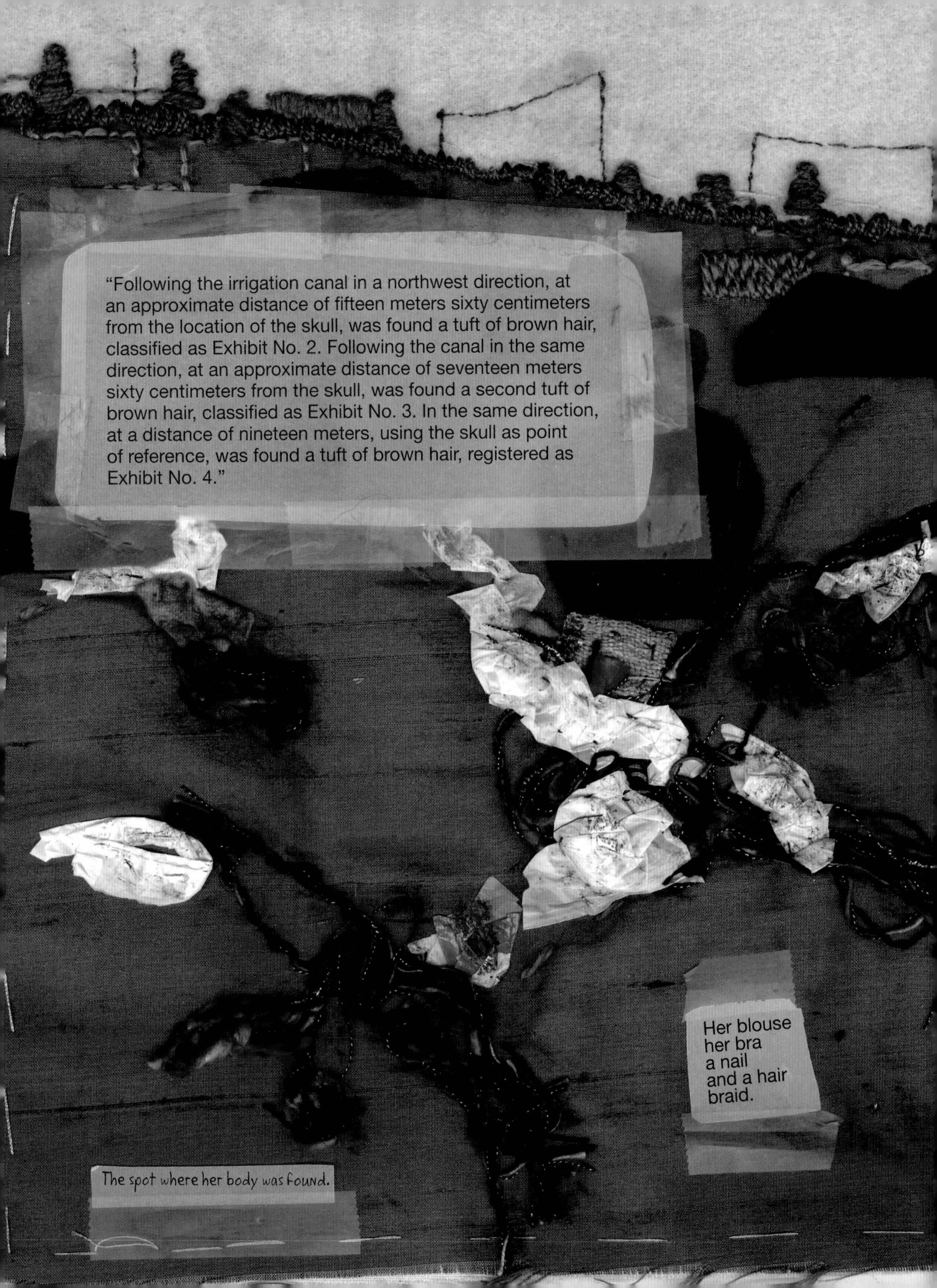
"Following the irrigation canal in a northwest direction, at an approximate distance of fifteen meters sixty centimeters from the location of the skull, was found a tuft of brown hair, classified as Exhibit No. 2. Following the canal in the same direction, at an approximate distance of seventeen meters sixty centimeters from the skull, was found a second tuft of brown hair, classified as Exhibit No. 3. In the same direction, at a distance of nineteen meters, using the skull as point of reference, was found a tuft of brown hair, registered as Exhibit No. 4."
Her blouse her bra a nail and a hair braid.
The spot where her body was found.

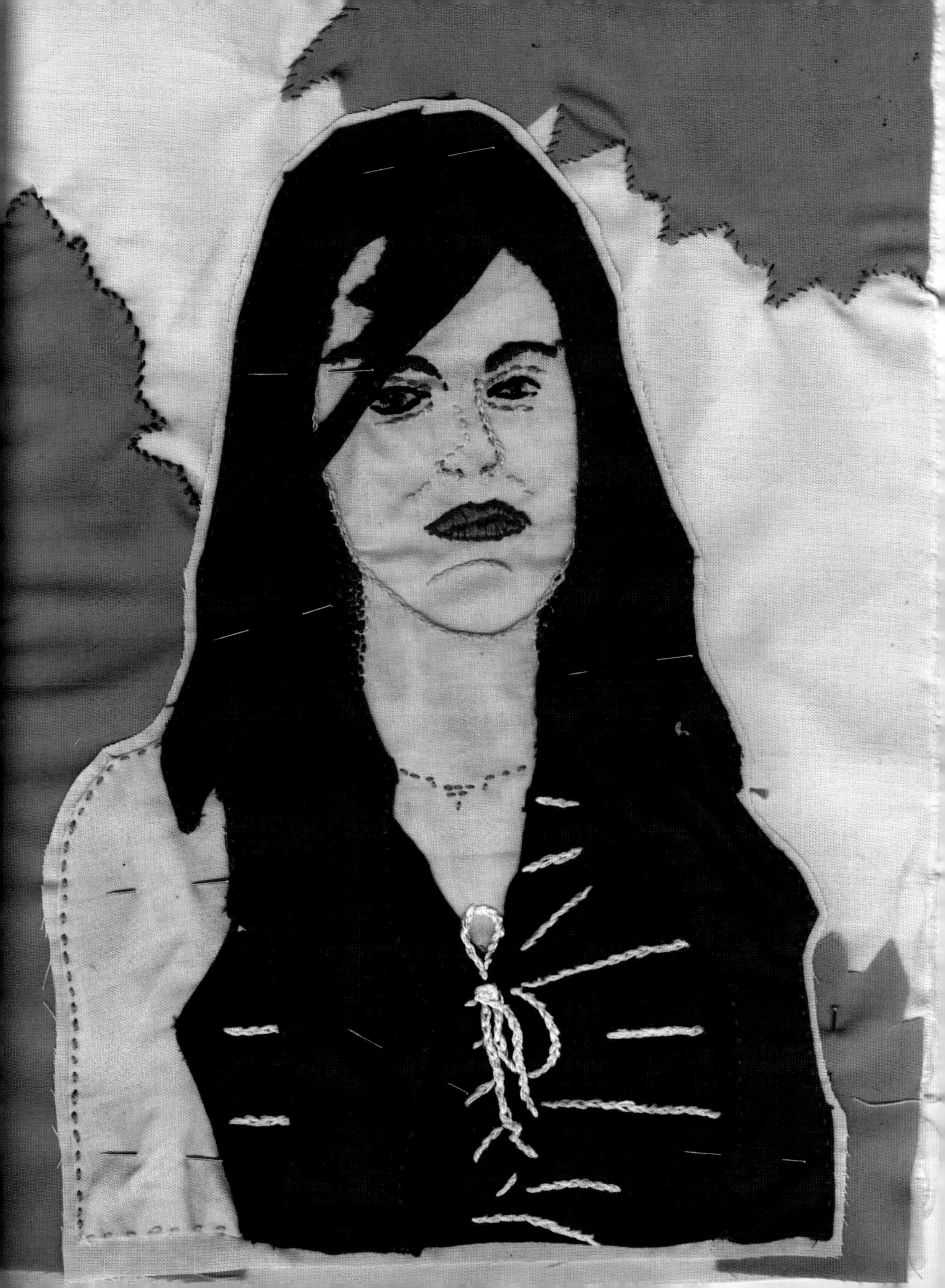

"She never really talked about her dad. I don't know. She didn't like that topic. I think that maybe it hurt her. All she said was that she didn't know him, and she didn't miss him."

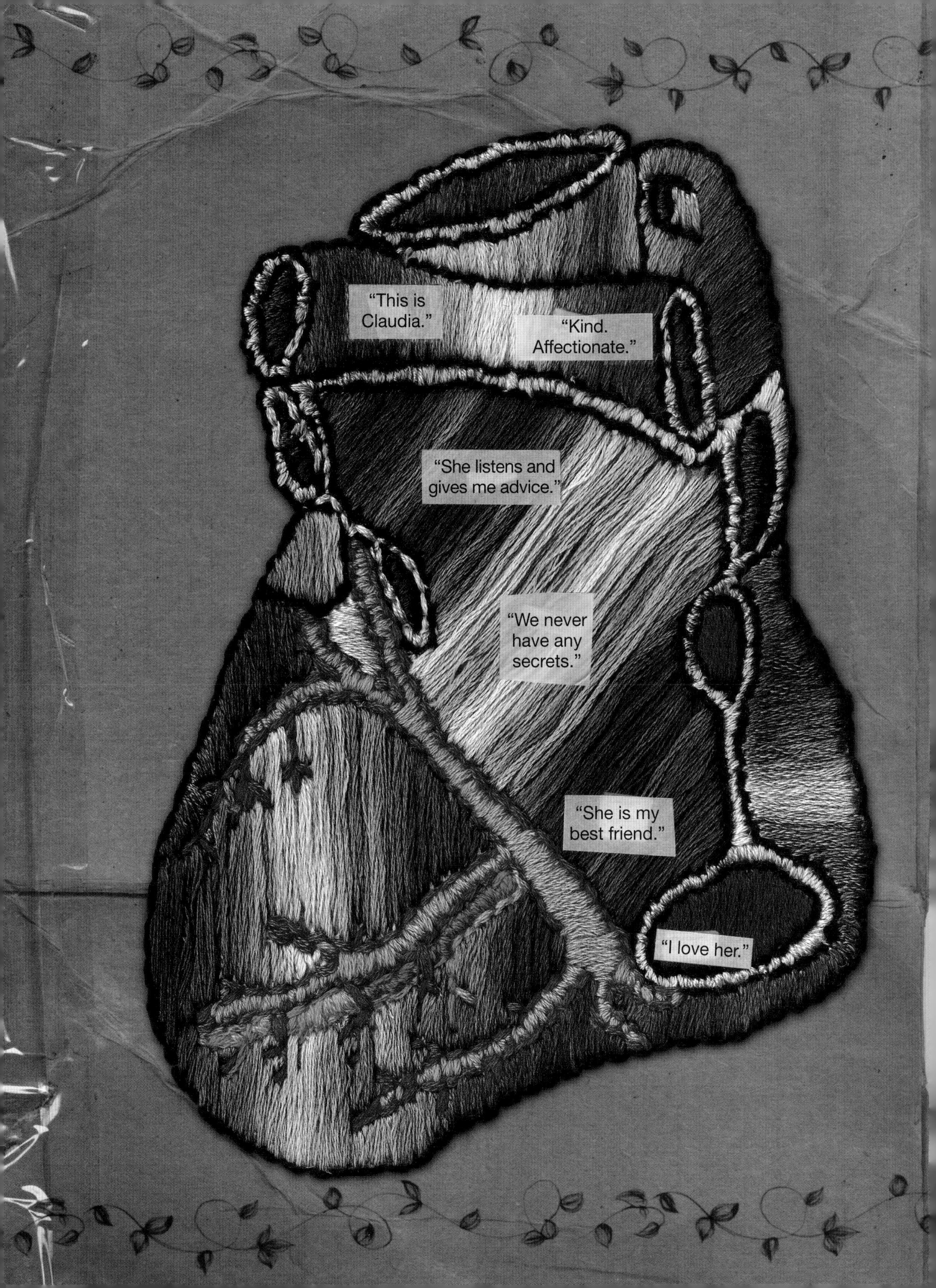
"This is Claudia."
"Kind. Affectionate."
"She listens and gives me advice."
"We never have any secrets."
"She is my best friend."
"I love her."

MARÍAELENAACOSTAARMENDÁRIZMARÍADELOS
AYRAGEMAALAMILLOGONZÁLEZNORMAPATRICI
OYOLANDAÁLVAREZESQUIHUAVIOLETAMABELA
ALAZARSILVIAARCEROSAMARGARITAARELLAN
RELLANOZUBIATEMARTHAARGUIJOCASTAÑEDA
REQUÍNMENDOZAROCÍOBARRAZAGALLEGOSSOL
JARRESANDORVERÓNICAGALVÁNMANJARESZEN
ERNÁNDEZGRACIELABUENODEHERNÁNDEZMART
AZAMORASAMANTHAYESENIACARRASCOCARRAS
CARRILLOENRÍQUEZOLGAALICIACARRILLOPE
ERÓNICACASTROPANDOANTONIACENICEROSCO
NACHÁVEZCALDERAANDORDESCONOCIDAESTEL
ÁNDEZCARLAMAGDALENACONTRERASLÓPEZMAR
CORDEROGARCÍAANDORDESCONOCIDAROSAISE
BERTAGEORGINACORONELMOLINAESTEFANIAC
ARROSAELIACUAZOZÓNMACHUCHOROSAINELAD
RADELAROSAMARTÍNEZPETRADELAROSAMOREN
ADELCASTILLOHOLGUÍNBRENDABERENICEDEL
NANCYJACQUELINEDONADOVÁZQUEZCATALINA
IDAGLORIANARÍAESCALANTERODRÍGUEZGLOR
OBEDOSOSAGUADALUPEIVONNEESTRADASALAS
GLADISJANETHFIDRROVARGASFATIMAVANESA
ÁTIMAFLORESORTÍZMARÍADELOSÁNGELESFRA
OFRANCISCAGALLARDOANDORFRANCISCALUCE
ÍADELOURDESGALVÁNJUÁREZELENAGARCÍAAL
ARCÍAANDRADEENMILIAGARCÍAHERNÁNDEZLU
IKAGARCÍAMORENOGRACIELAGARCÍAPRIMERO
ÁLASANDORMARÍATERESAGARCÍASALASMIRIA
REELENAGAUDINASIMENTALCELIAGUADALUPE
DELACRUZNELLYAMÉRICAGÓMEZOLGUÍNMARÍA
ÁLEZLORENZAISELAGONZÁLEZALAMILLOMARÍ
LEZGUTIÉRREZOLGAGONZÁLEZLÓPEZTERESAD
ÓNKARINADANIELAGUTIÉRREZSANDRACORINA
ÉRREZPORTILLOLOURDESGUTIÉRREZROSALES
ARÍAISABELHAROPRADOMANUELAHERMOSILLO
ÍAAGUSTINAHERNÁNDEZROSAVIRGINIAHERNÁ
ÍADELALUZHERNÁNDEZCHÁVEZELBAHERNÁNDE
HERRERAMONREALTERESAELIDAHERRERAREYA
AGOVERÓNICEHUITRÓNQUEZADAANDORDESCON
LAITUARTESILVAESMERALDAJUÁREZALARCÓN
AGUNACRUZLAURAROCÍOLARAAMAROREINASAR
ROSALEÓNRAMOSROSAMARÍALERMAHERNÁNDEZ

GELESACOSTARAMIREZANDORDESCONOCIDAM
LBARIOSMARIADELOSANGELESALVARADOSOT
IDREZBARRIOSMARIAASCENSIONAPARICIOS
GARCIAIRMAARELLANOCASTILLOVICTORIAA
TICIAARMEMDARIZCHAVIRAELSAAMERICAAR
ADBELTRANCASTILLOVERONICABELTRANMAN
DABERMUDEZCAMPAMIRIAMGLIZETHBERNALH
FELICIACAMPOSMOLINAMARIAMAURACARMON
ELVIRACARRILLODELATORREERICKANOHEMI
ZMARIALUISACARSOLIBERUMENGUADALUPEV
ALALMAMIREYACHAVARRIAFAVILAMARIAELE
HAVEZGARDEAMARIATERESACONTRERASHERN
DELROCIOCORDEROESQUIVELLAURALOURDES
CORONASANTOSANDORROSAISELACARMONARO
RALGONZALEZCECILILACOVARRUBIASAGUIL
ACRUZMADRIGALIVONNEDELAOGARCIATEODO
ARIASATURNINADELEONCALAMACOALEJANDR
DORODRIGUEZGABRIELADOMINGUEZAGUILAR
ARTECARRERA"ELIZABETH"ANDORDESCONOC
ELENAESCOBEDOPIÑAREDECAELIZABETHESC
LTAFIERROELIASAPOLONIAFIERROPOBLANO
ORESDIAZROSAISELAFLORESGARCIAMARIAF
MARTINEZLILIANAFRAYREBUSTILLOSLUCER
GALLARDOARACELIGALLARDORODRIGUEZMAR
RADOANDORDESCONOCIDALILIAALEJANDRAG
AGARCIAHERNANDEZROSARIOGARCIALEALER
TICIAGARCIAROSALESMARIAELENAGARCIAS
ARCIASOLORIOBLANCAESTHELAGARZAAGUIR
MEZDELACRUZANDORCELIAGUADALUPELOPEZ
LROSARIOGOMEZSOLISCLAUDIAIVETTEGONZ
AGRARIOGONZALEZFLORESROSAMARIAGONZA
JESUSGONZALEZMENDOZAJUANAGONZALEZPIN
TIERREZESTRADAMARIADELOSANGELESGUTIM
ANCAGRISELGUZMANAMPAROGUZMANCAIXBAM
EZADAFRANCISCAEPIGMENIAHERNANDEZMAR
EZCANOGUILLERMINAHERNANDEZCHAVEZMAR
ARTINEZLIDIAHERRBRAHERRERAESMERALDA
HIPOLITOCAMPOSLILIANAHOLGUINDESANTI
IDAPAULINAIBARRADELEONROSAMARIAMAYE
NDRALUZJUAREZVAZQUEZSILVIAGABRIELAL
LARALUCIANORAQUELLECHUGAMACIASMARIA
MERALDALEYVARODRIGUEZROSALBILOPEZES

PINOZAANDORDESCONOCIDAALMAMARGARITALU
OZANOBOLAÑOSLOURDESIVETTELUCEROCAMPOS
ONOCIDAMARIAJULIALUNAVERAANGELICALUN
ELIMANRIQUEZGOMEZIRMAMARQUEZANGELICAM
LIAMARQUEZVALENZUELALAURAALONDRAMARQ
NGELEDITHGABRIELAMARTINEZCALVILLOMAR
NEZHERNANDEZANDORDESCONOCIDAMARIAEUG
ZARACELYESMERALDAMARTINEZMONTAÑEZYES
NEZRAMOSANDORDESCONOCIDALUZADRIANAMA
MARIAESTELAMARTINEZVALDEZISABELMEJIA
AEUGENIAMENDOZAARIASNATIVIDADMONCLOA
CIAMORALESSOTOFLOREMILIAMONREALMELEN
MUÑOZANDRADEMARIADELALUZMURGADOGUTIE
EJESUSNAVARRETEREYESBRISIAJANETHNEVA
DELREFUGIONUÑEZLOPEZARACELYNUÑEZSANTO
ASKARLALIZETHOVIEDORODRIGUEZLORENAAN
UIRREROSAIVONNEPAEZMARQUEZROSAMARTHA
EZMARIADELROSARIOPALACIOSMORANPATRIC
LAUDIAPIZARROVELAZQUEZERENDIRAIVONNE
DORANTONIARAMIREZCALDERONMARIASANTOS
KARINACANDELARIARAMOSGONZALEZCLAUDIA
NDORDESCONOCIDAMARIADELROSARIORAMOSR
ARENTERIASALAZARELBARESENDIZRODRIGUE
ESPINOSAMAYRAJULIANAREYESSOLISANDORDE
IARIVASMARTINEZROSAMARIARIVERABARAJA
ODRIGUEZELIZABETHROBLESGOMEZELIZABET
EZSAENZIRMAANGELICAROSALESLOZANODAIS
RIAMSOLEDADSAENZRIVERAARGELIASALAZAR
ESUSSANDOVALGONZALEZJUANSANDOVALREYN
ASANTOSVARGASAMALIAMARIADELOSDOLORES
ASTROINESSILVAMERCHANTLUCILASILVASAL
ATAPIAVEGACLAUDIAIVETTETAVARESRIVERA
FLORBSFRANCISCATORRESCASILLASADRIANA
IAYARELITORRESTORRESDOMITILATRUJILLO
AZQUEZANTONIAVALLESFUENTESSUZZANEVAN
ESLAURAGEORGINAVARGASLETICIAVARGASFL
ETELAVAZQUEZVALENZUELAMARTHAESMERALDA
PATAALVAREZMARIASALUDZENDEJASMARTINE
ADESCONOCIDADESCONOCIDADESCONOCIDADE
OCIDADESCONOCIDADESCONOCIDADESCONOCI
SCONOCIDADESCONOCIDADESCONOCIDADESCO
DADESCONOCIDADESCONOCIDADESCONOCIDAD
NOCIDADESCONOCIDADESCONOCIDADESCONOC
ESCONOCIDADESCONOCIDADESCONOCIDADESCO

EZGARZAMARIALOPEZTORRESAIDAARACELIL
LUCY"GUADALUPELUNADELAROSAANDORDESC
ILLALOBOSMARCELAMACIASHERNANDEZARAC
RQUEZLEDEZMAANDORDESCONOCIDAFLORIDA
ZVALENZUELAROSARIODEFATIMAMARTINEZA
ISABELMARTINEZGONZALEZVERONICAMARTI
IAMARTINEZJOOADRIANAMARTINEZMARTINE
AMARTINEZMORALESBARBARAARACELIMARTI
INEZREYESELIZABETHMARTINEZRODRIGUEZ
PIENBRENDAPATRICIAMENDEZVAZQUEZMARI
RENOMARIADELALUZMORALESCOHETEROIGNA
ZNORMALETICIAMORENOQUINTEROVERONICA
EZMARIAISABELNAVAVAZQUEZMARIACELIAD
SDELOSSANTOSGEMMAGARCIANEVAREZMARIA
,SILVIAOCONLOPEZCONSUELOORTIZCONTRER
LICAOVIEDORODRIGUEZMARIAINESOZUNAAG
LACIOSBRIONESNORMAMAYELAPALACIOSLOP
AKA"LABURRA"ELODIAPAYANNUÑEZMARTHAC
NCEHERNANDEZMARIACRISTINAQUEZADAAMA
MIREZVEGAGLADYSLIZETHRAMOSESCARZAGA
MOSLOPEZLAURABERENICERAMOSMONARREZA
ESMARIASANTOSRANGELFLORESMARIATERES
ETICIAREYESBENITEZLILIAJULIANAREYES
SCONOCIDABLANCACECILIARIVASLOPEZGLOR
ILVIAELENARIVERAMORALESELISARIVERAR
RODRIGUEZPEREZMERLINELIZABETHRODRIGU
UEDASALCIDOPERLAPATRICIASAENZDIAZMIJ
ISPINMARIAELENASALCEDOMERAZMARIADEJ
MARIAVERONICASANTELLANEZNAJERAMARCEL
UCEDODIAZDELEONIRMAREBECASIFUENTESC
ASKARINASOTODIAZ"TANIA"GLORIAYOLAND
SAISELATENAQUINTANILLAMARISATORIBIO
RRESMARQUEZVIRIDIANATORRESMORENOSON
SADAESMERALDAURIASSAENZCELINAURIBEV
EROPHESTERBEATRIZANGELICAVARELAFLOR
ESMIRIAMARLEMVAZQUEZMENDOZABLANCAESA
LOZVALDEZALEJANDRAVIEZCASTROCLARAZA
AULAZEPEDAMENADESCONOCIDADESCONOCID
ONOCIDADESCONOCIDADESCONOCIDADESCON
DESCONOCIDADESCONOCIDADESCONOCIDADE
CIDADESCONOCIDADESCONOCIDADESCONOCI
CONOCIDADESCONOCIDADESCONOCIDADESCO
ADESCONOCIDADESCONOCIDADESCONOCIDAD
OCIDADESCONOCIDADESCONOCIDADESCONOC

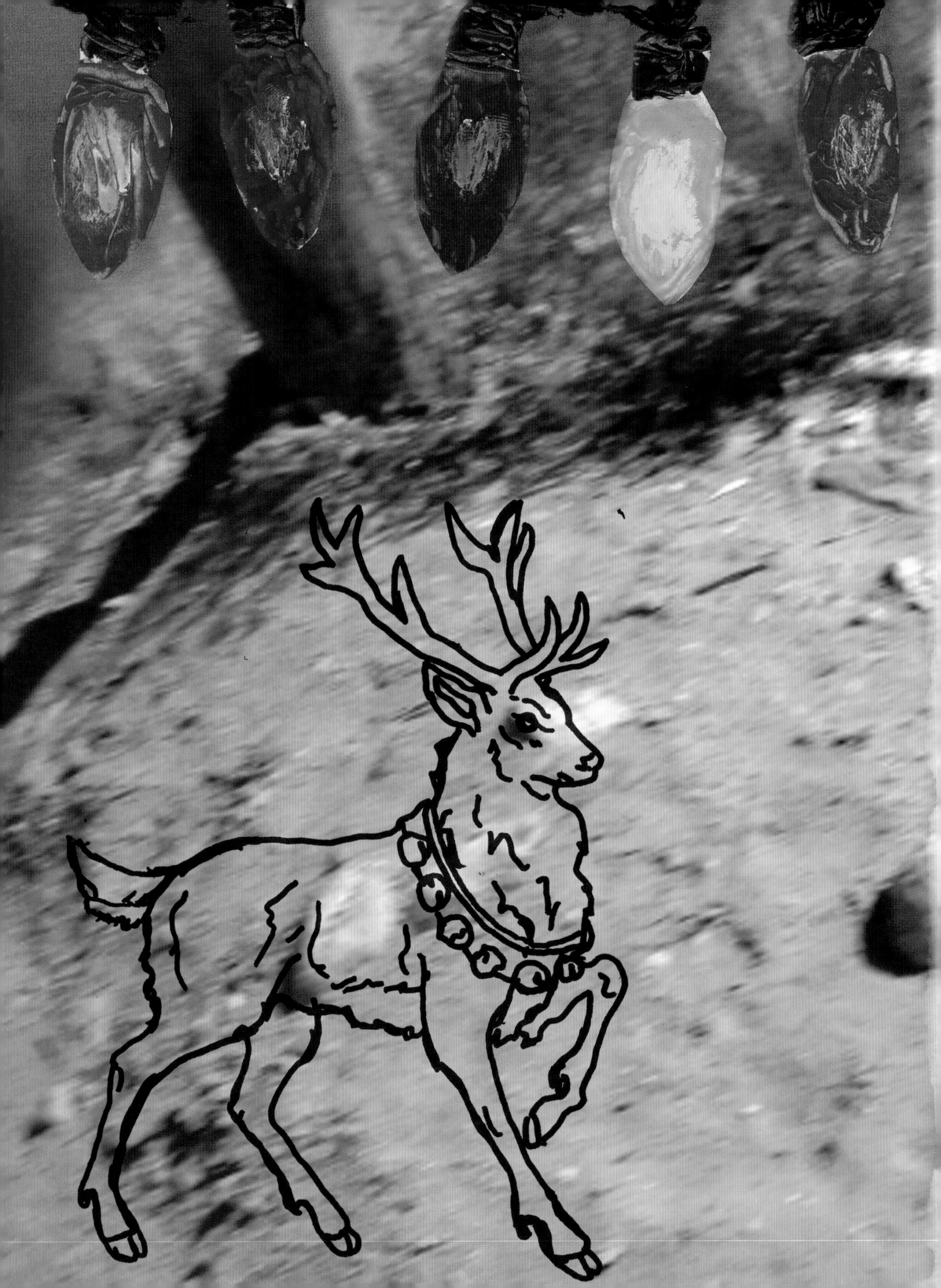

The cotton field. I didn't want to see it.

On my last day in Juárez, I go there with my video camera. The field is in the middle of a busy intersection. Cars speed by and buses labor along the pavement. How did someone dump eight bodies in here without anyone noticing? It's right across the street from the offices of the Association of Maquiladoras. On the edge of the field, I notice a police surveillance van idling. I step across the cracked earth, over broken beer bottles and discarded shoes. My translator hangs a few steps behind me, perhaps afraid that we might get in trouble for being here. There is nothing but debris.

Juárez and the U.S. are separated by a stream that runs below the bridge. Driving across, we get caught in a traffic jam. All along the balustrade, teenage boys hand out flyers for Wal-Mart and Blockbuster. A girl who looks seventeen sells cotton candy while a baby sleeps in her arms. The car is hot. We're listening to hip-hop, then lots of radio commercials, then trumpet music that's quiet and then explodes from the speakers like a jack-in-the-box. Why does my translator keep turning up the volume when the commercials come on? Suddenly a man is pounding on our front window. He holds his hand out for money and rolls up his sleeve. There are track marks that foam with pus and blood. It takes over an hour to cross into America.

And then we are in a suburb. We stop in a mall for lunch, where Christmas music is piping over the speakers. Every store window is filled with a Christmas display. Reindeer in gold bells pull the sleigh of presents. I'm in a jeans store when a poster near the changing room catches my eye. On it, an African American man is laughing and rolling a snowball next to a redhead girl with smooth hair. Snow is caught in her eyelashes and fuzzy sweater, her cheeks red like pomegranates. I feel like an alien.

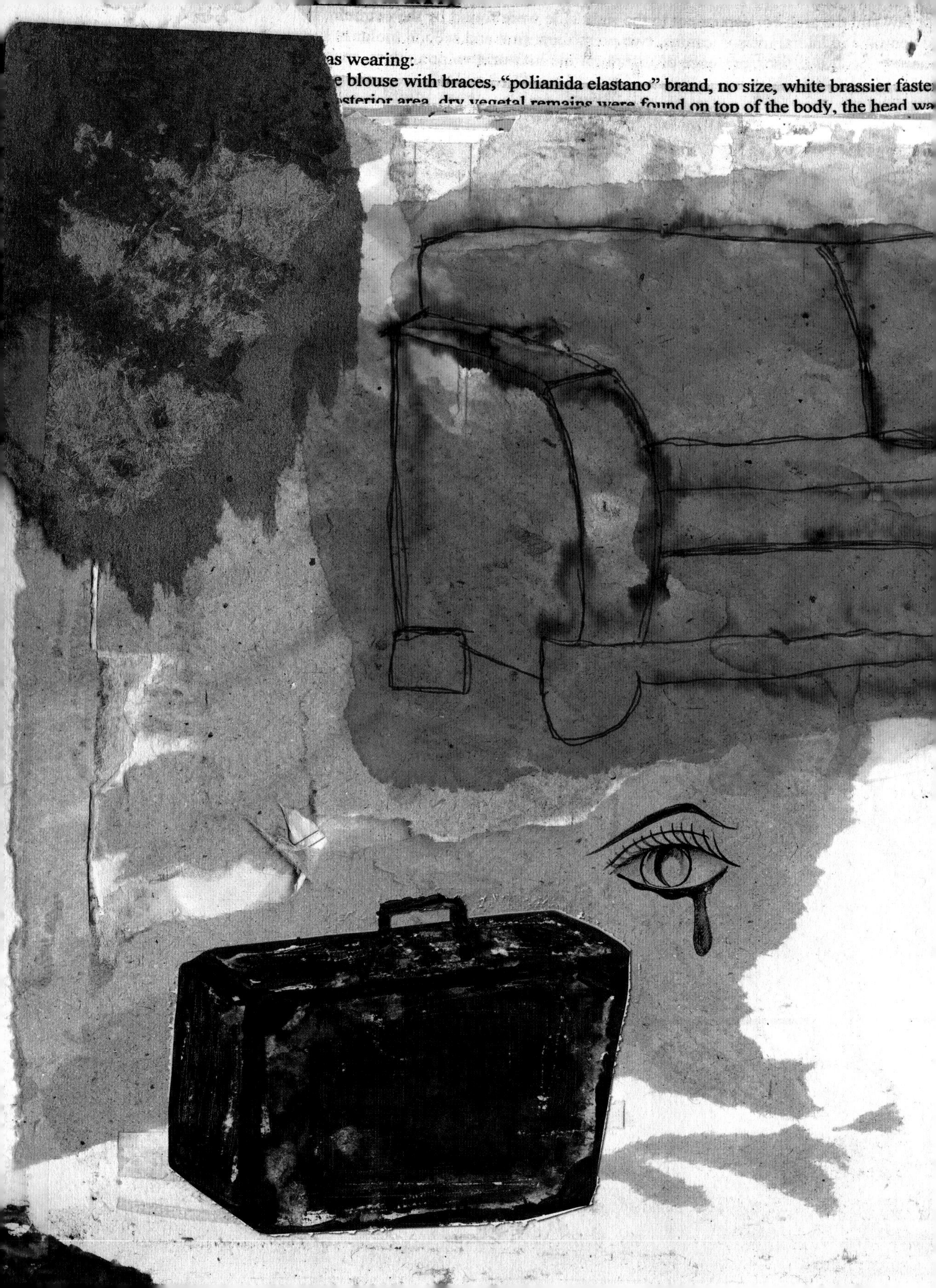
as wearing:
e blouse with braces, “polianida elastano” brand, no size, white brassier faste
sterior area, dry vegetal remains were found on top of the body, the head wa

CRANIUM

Emaciated with bruise to the bone tissue level; presence of cranium sutures. The superior dental arch, presented in the right side, a canine, one and two premolar, first molar and part of the second molar, absence of central and lateral incisors. In the left side, it presented a canine, two premolars, first molar with silver socket, second molar with

It starts at the airport and goes on for weeks. That middle-of-the-night sobbing that stops suddenly and you fall asleep only to be overwhelmed again in some random place like a pet store.

I came home from Juárez with photos, a bag of dirt from the cotton field, writing from the families, autopsy reports. All of this material sits on my couch like visiting guests for tea. I can't touch it.

The deaths are savage. I don't know how to answer any of the questions the families have been asking for more than ten years. Juárez, you won. I've choked.

I decide to go home to Toronto. I miss my family.

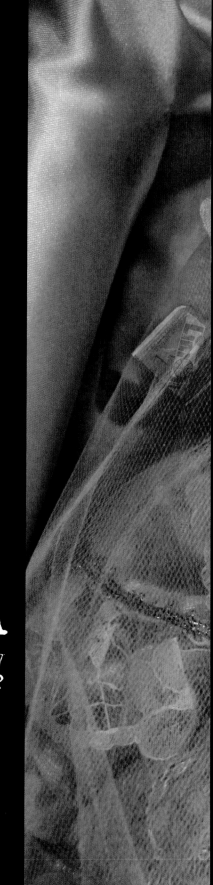

LA TRISTEZA

Has anyone supposed it lucky
to be born?

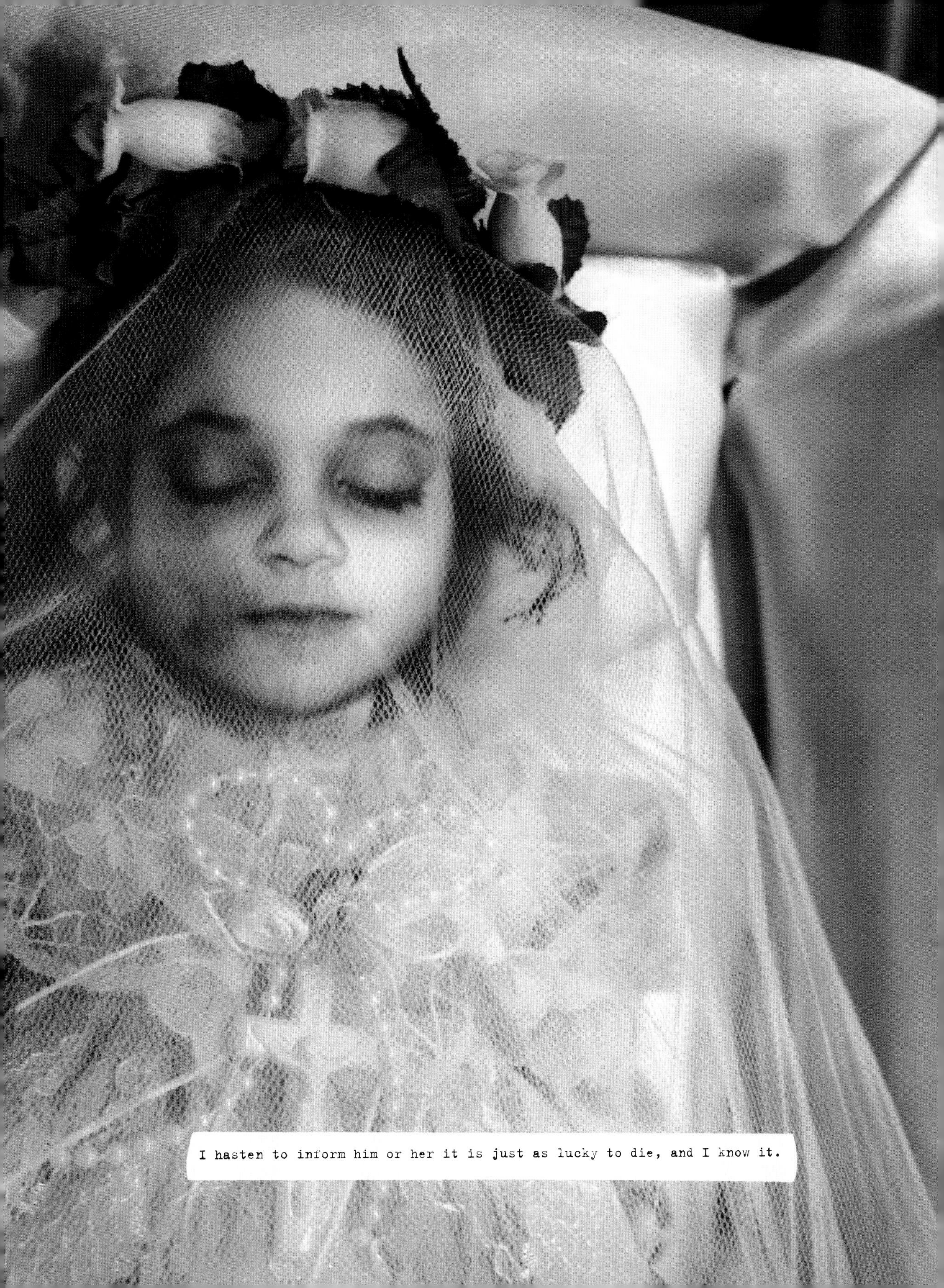

I hasten to inform him or her it is just as lucky to die, and I know it.

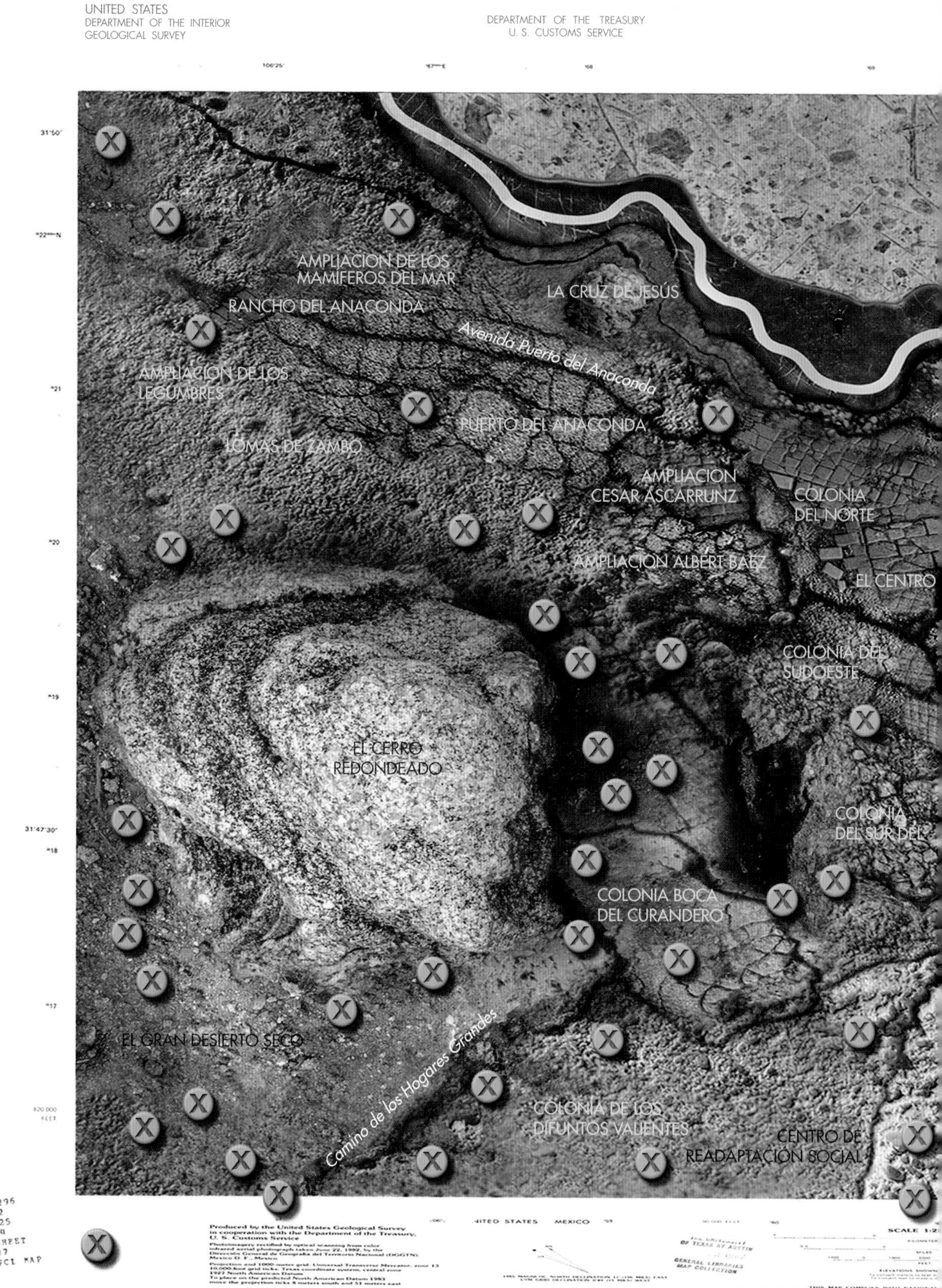
UNITED STATES
DEPARTMENT OF THE INTERIOR
GEOLOGICAL SURVEY
DEPARTMENT OF THE TREASURY
U. S. CUSTOMS SERVICE
106°25'
31°50'
31°47'30"
AMPLIACION DE LOS
MAMIFEROS DEL MAR
LA CRUZ DE JESÚS
RANCHO DEL ANACONDA
Avenida Puerto del Anaconda
AMPLIACION DE LOS
LEGUMBRES
PUERTO DEL ANACONDA
LOMAS DE ZAMBO
AMPLIACION
CESAR ASCARRUNZ
COLONIA
DEL NORTE
AMPLIACION ALBERT BAEZ
EL CENTRO
COLONIA DEL
SUDOESTE
EL CERRO
REDONDEADO
COLONIA
DEL SUR DEL
COLONIA BOCA
DEL CURANDERO
EL GRAN DESIERTO SECO
Camino de los Hogares Grandes
COLONIA DE LOS
DIFUNTOS VALIENTES
CENTRO DE
READAPTACIÓN SOCIAL
UNITED STATES MEXICO
Produced by the United States Geological Survey
in cooperation with the Department of the Treasury,
U. S. Customs Service
Photoimagery rectified by optical scanning from color
infrared aerial photograph taken June 22, 1992, by the
Dirección General de Geografía del Territorio Nacional (DGGTN),
Mexico D. F., Mexico
Projection and 1000-meter grid: Universal Transverse Mercator, zone 13
10,000-foot grid ticks: Texas coordinate system, central zone
1927 North American Datum
To place on the predicted North American Datum 1983
move the projection ticks 8 meters south and 51 meters east
SCALE 1:2
THE UNIVERSITY
OF TEXAS AT AUSTIN
GENERAL LIBRARIES
MAP COLLECTION
THIS MAP COMPLIES WITH NATIONAL
FOR SALE BY U. S. GEOLOGICAL SURVEY, DENVER,
AND BY CENTRO DE ASESORIA Y VENTA DE INF
BALDERAS #71, MEZZANI

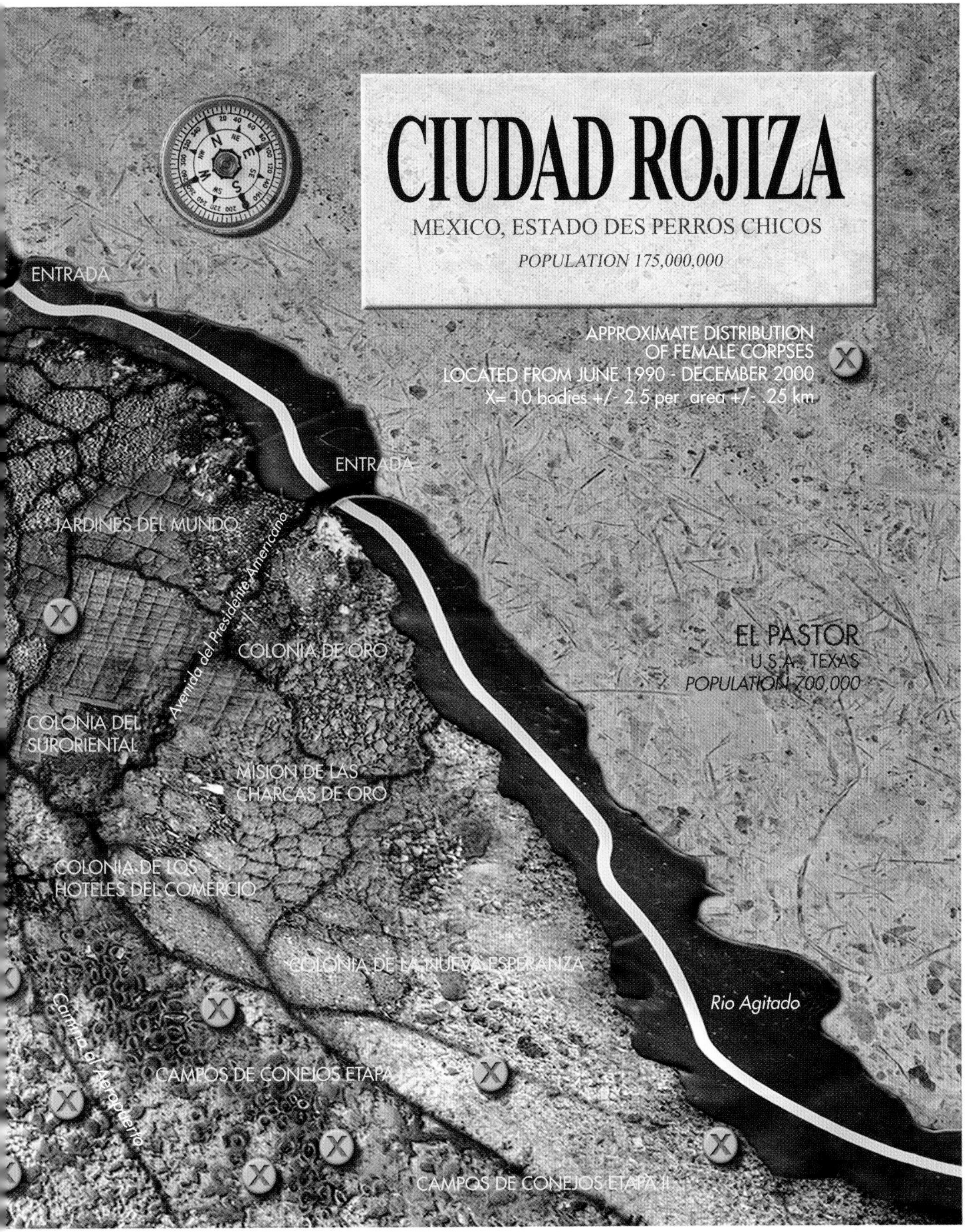
CIUDAD ROJIZA
MEXICO, ESTADO DES PERROS CHICOS
POPULATION 175,000,000
ENTRADA
APPROXIMATE DISTRIBUTION
OF FEMALE CORPSES
LOCATED FROM JUNE 1990 - DECEMBER 2000
X= 10 bodies +/- 2.5 per area +/- .25 km
ENTRADA
JARDINES DEL MUNDO
Avenida del Presidente Americano
COLONIA DE ORO
EL PASTOR
U.S.A., TEXAS
POPULATION 700,000
COLONIA DEL
SURORIENTAL
MISION DE LAS
CHARCAS DE ORO
COLONIA DE LOS
HOTELES DEL COMERCIO
COLONIA DE LA NUEVA ESPERANZA
Rio Agitado
Camino al Aeropuerto
CAMPOS DE CONEJOS ETAPA I
CAMPOS DE CONEJOS ETAPA II

UNITED STATES

MEXICO

31°42'30"

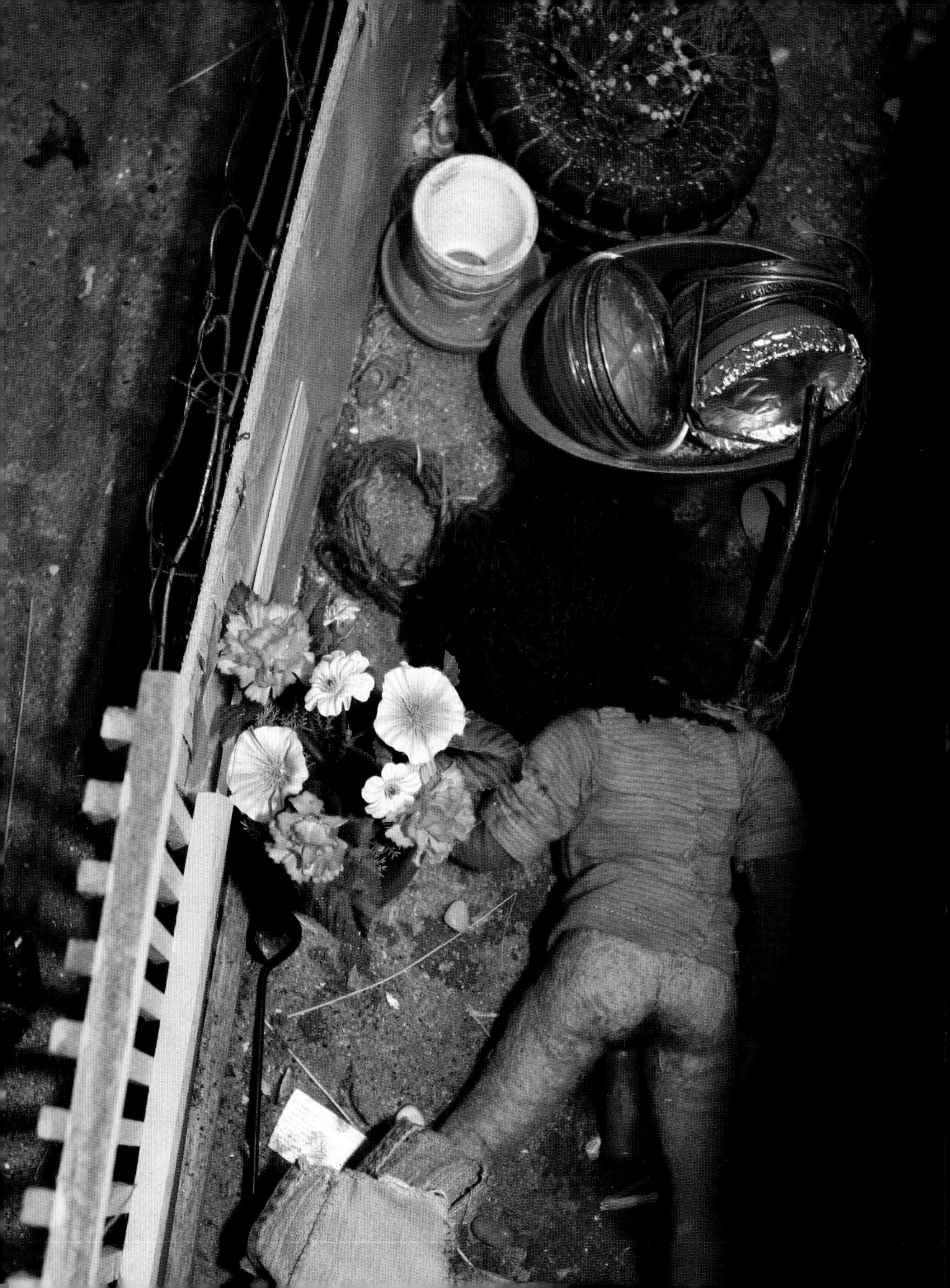

THE NEWS OF 17 FEBRUARY

CAMPOS DE CONEJOS ETAPA I

MINOR FOUND WITHOUT LIFE

A person who was a young woman was found passed away, thrown to several meters of her house.

During the first investigations several signalings of neighbors and the own family of the adolescent were obtained, and it was found out a neighbor bothered it constantly.

Its neighbor finished confessing the commission of the crime while he was lengthy in the facilities of the office of the public prosecutor.

The assassin explained that he killed the minor, who was sixteen years old, because this one made fun frequently of him, saying to him that the wife deceived it with other men and therefore he was "cornudo."

He did not further support these insults that the adolescent did to him, reason why he ended up cutting the neck deeply outside the house where the victim lived.

He first attacked the minor and introduced to him in her intimate parts a piece of wood to make tortillas. The assassin filled the wood object with dental paste, to lubricant to introduce it to the woman. This not typical like violation crime, that implies the introduction of the viril member with the absence of the consent of the affected person.

The man added for that he is sorry to have to committed the crime, and that if it could return the time never would think about killing a human being.

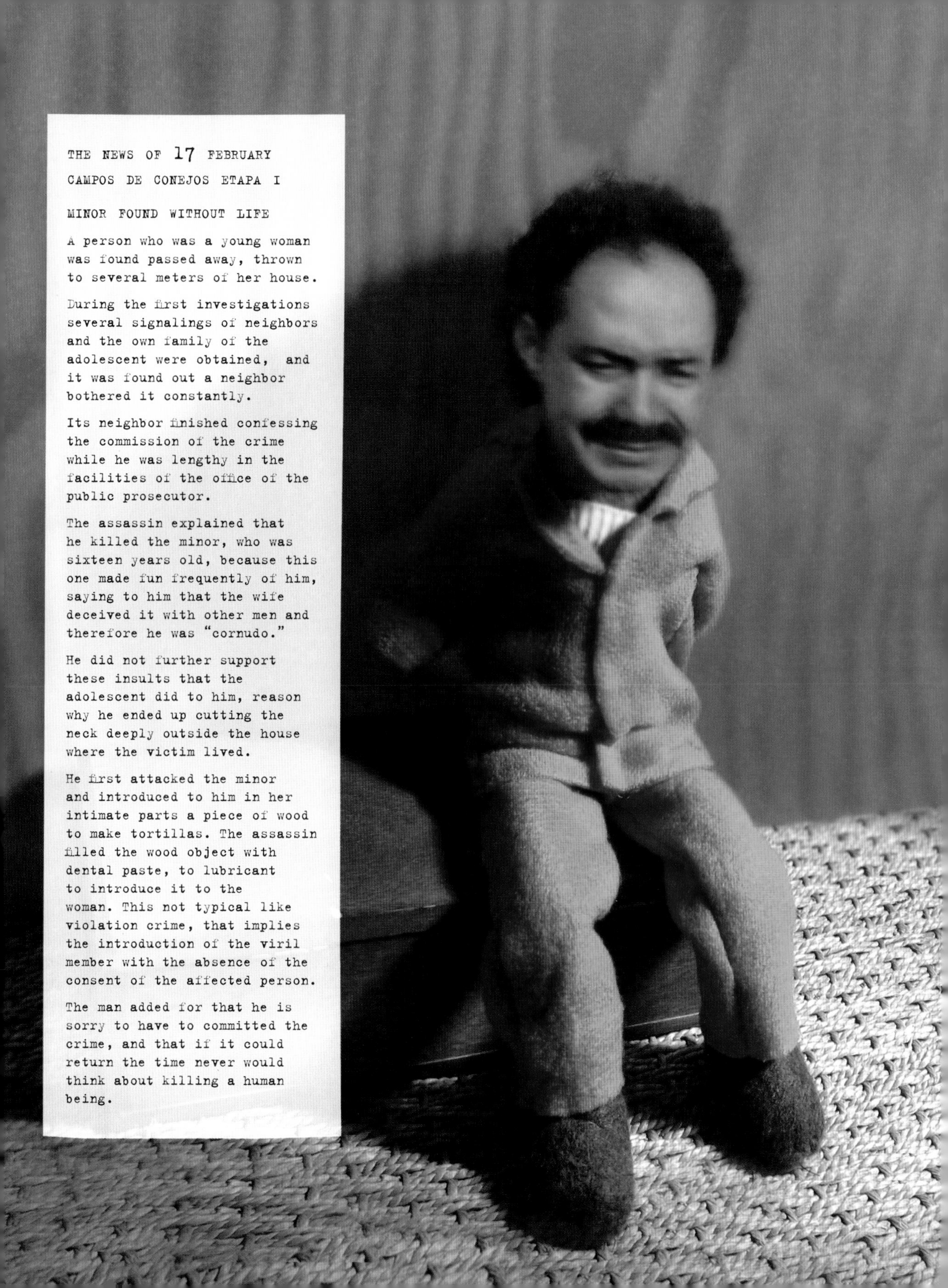

THE NEWS OF THE BORDER AREA

3 AUGUST

The confessions of the members of the group indicated that there never were less than of two men in each one of the girls at any time and that they violated to them oral, anal, and vaginally for the whole hour. One of the members of group said for the moment at which he obtained to one of the girls, "it was loose and sloppy." One other of the men was boasted to have "virginal blood" on him.

When the violations finished, the members of the group took the girls from the clear area to an area with strewings. A girl was strangled with her belt, and when it broke herself, the man G—— stomped in its neck, complaining that "that the dog will not die."

They strangled to the other girl with its shoe cords, after crying and to request for not being killed. In useless, she tried to deal with the men, offering to give her phone number so they will "meet again."

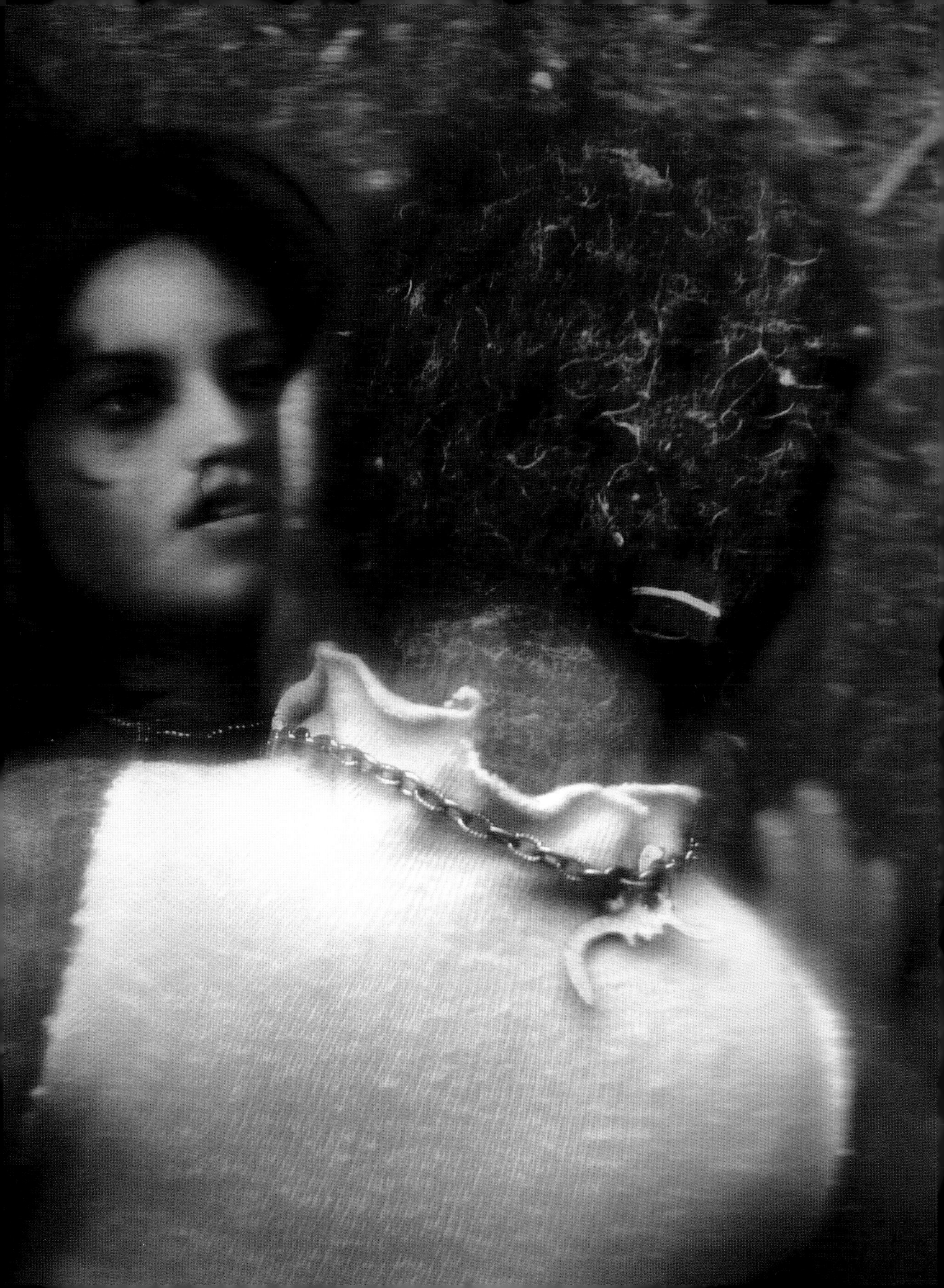

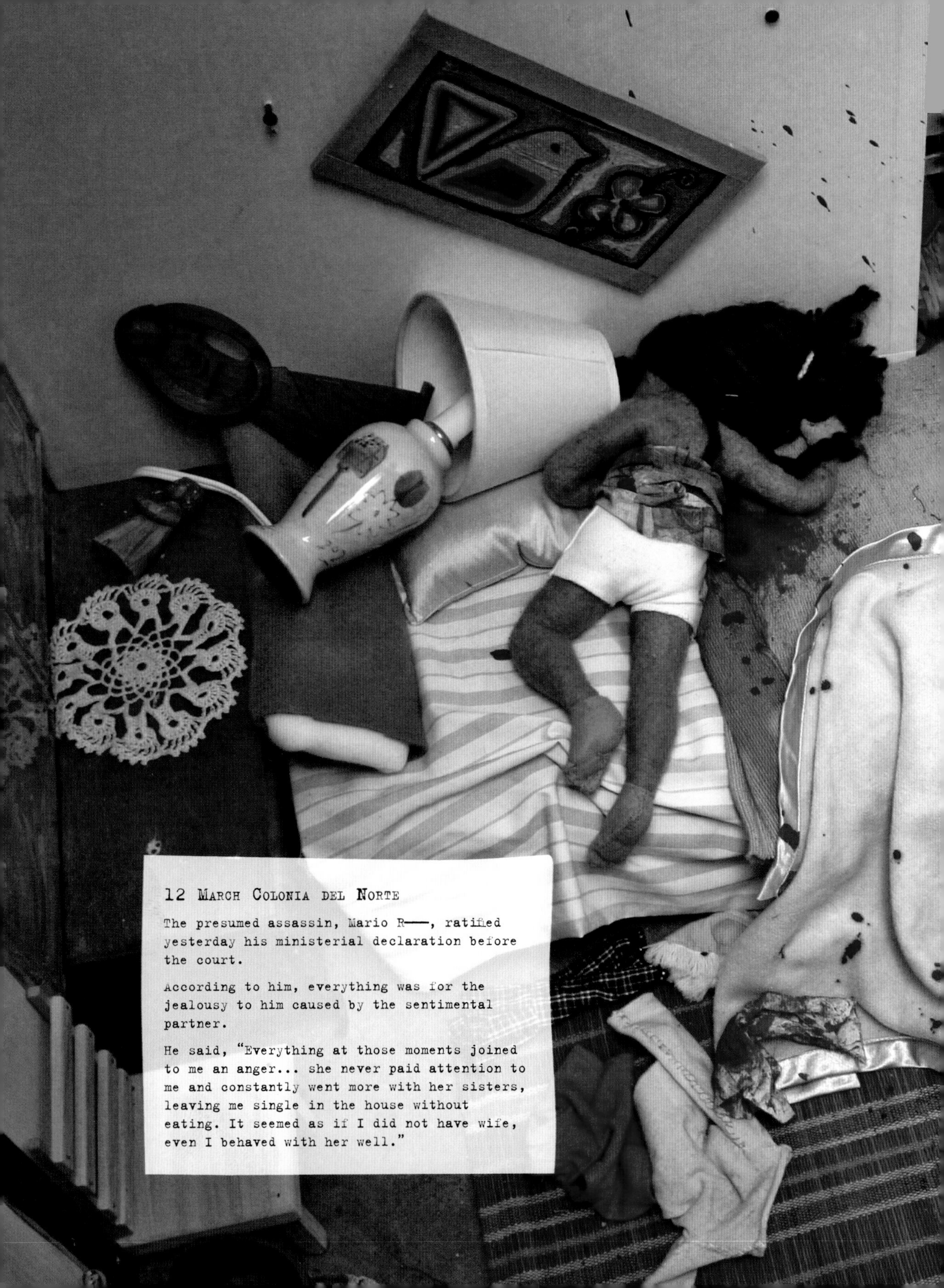

12 March Colonia del Norte

The presumed assassin, Mario R——, ratified yesterday his ministerial declaration before the court.

According to him, everything was for the jealousy to him caused by the sentimental partner.

He said, "Everything at those moments joined to me an anger... she never paid attention to me and constantly went more with her sisters, leaving me single in the house without eating. It seemed as if I did not have wife, even I behaved with her well."

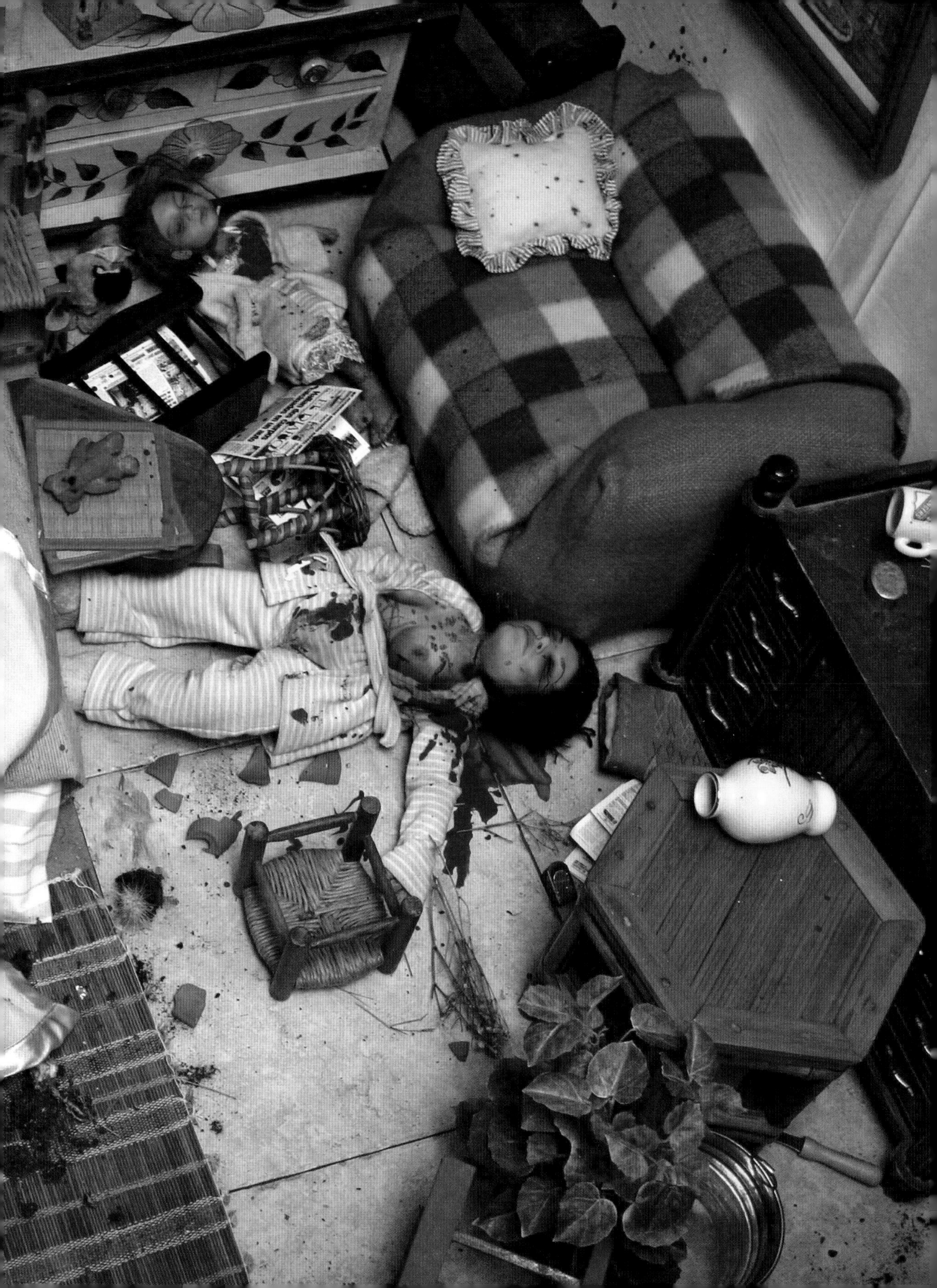

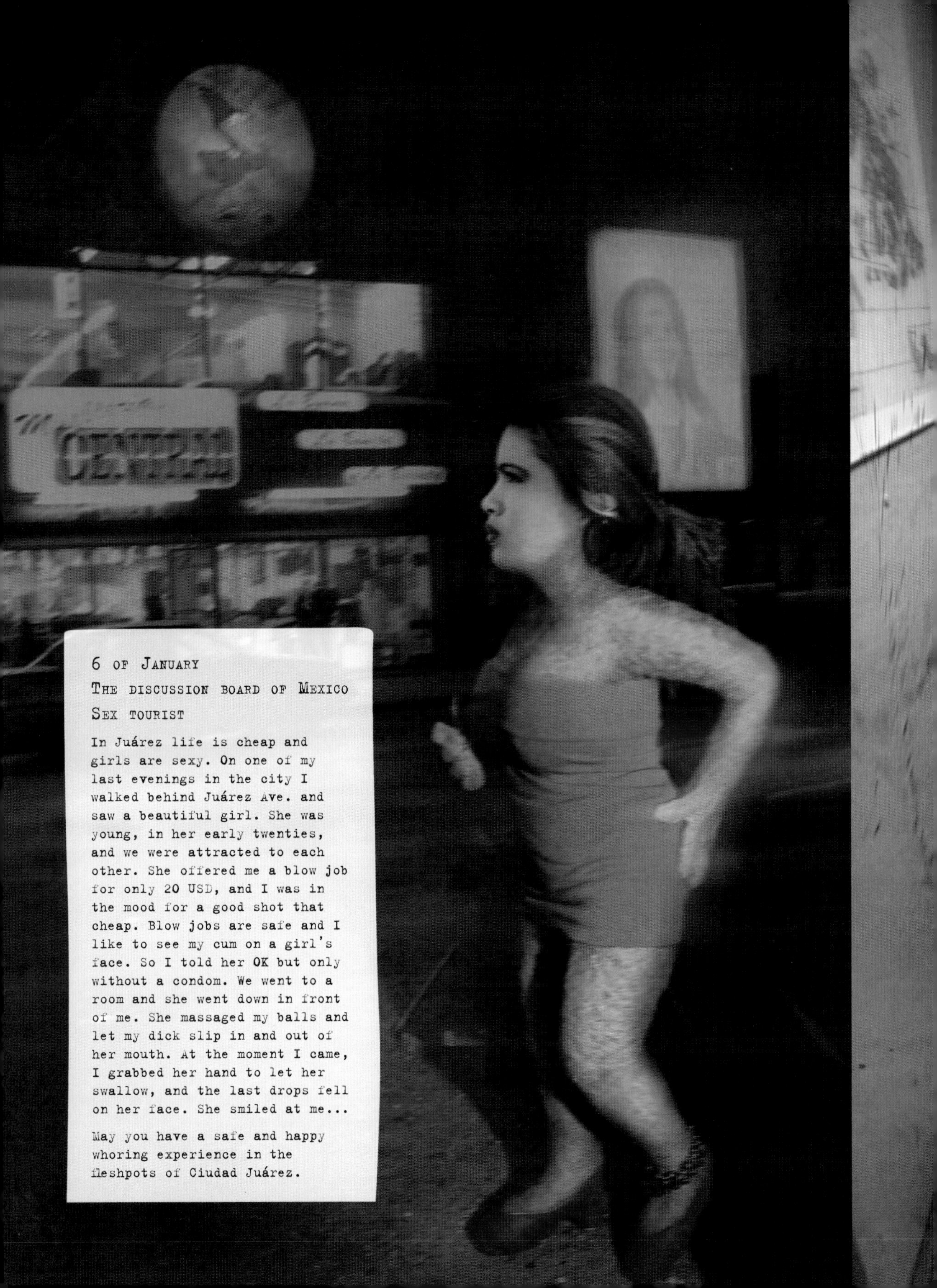
CENTRAL

6 of January

The discussion board of Mexico

Sex tourist

In Juárez life is cheap and girls are sexy. On one of my last evenings in the city I walked behind Juárez Ave. and saw a beautiful girl. She was young, in her early twenties, and we were attracted to each other. She offered me a blow job for only 20 USD, and I was in the mood for a good shot that cheap. Blow jobs are safe and I like to see my cum on a girl's face. So I told her OK but only without a condom. We went to a room and she went down in front of me. She massaged my balls and let my dick slip in and out of her mouth. At the moment I came, I grabbed her hand to let her swallow, and the last drops fell on her face. She smiled at me...

May you have a safe and happy whoring experience in the fleshpots of Ciudad Juárez.

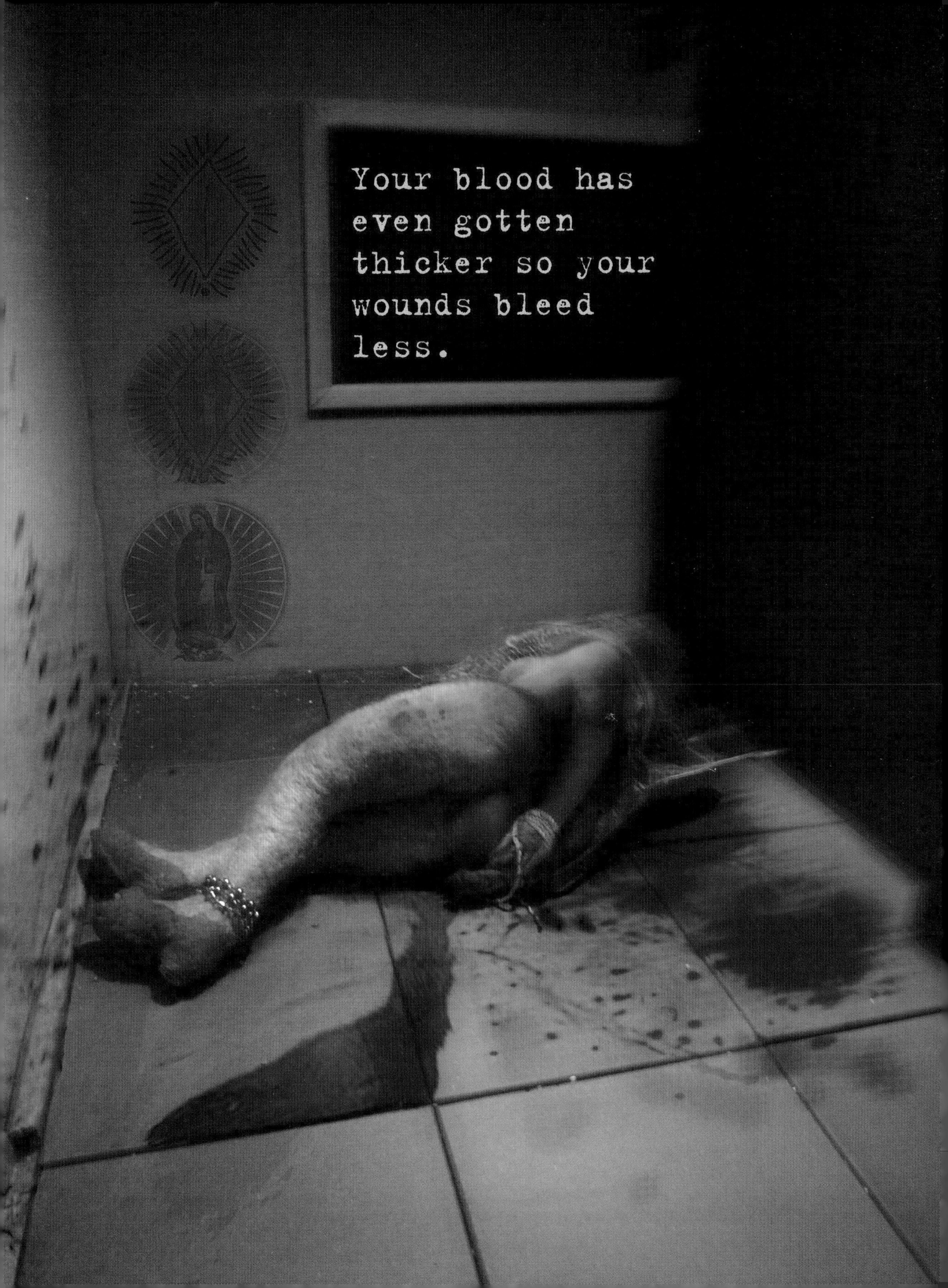
Your blood has even gotten thicker so your wounds bleed less.

He only knew of death what all men may:
that those it takes it thrusts into dumb night.
When she herself, though, —no, not snatched away,
But tenderly unloosened from his sight,

had glided over to unknown shades,
and when he felt that he had now resigned
the moonlight of her laughter to their glades,
and all her ways of being kind:

then all at once he came to understand
the dead through her, and joined them in their walk,
kin to them all; he let the others talk,

and paid no heed to them, and called that land
the fortunately-placed, the ever-sweet.—
And groped out all its pathways for her feet.

the Beloved"
lke, tr. J. B. Leishman

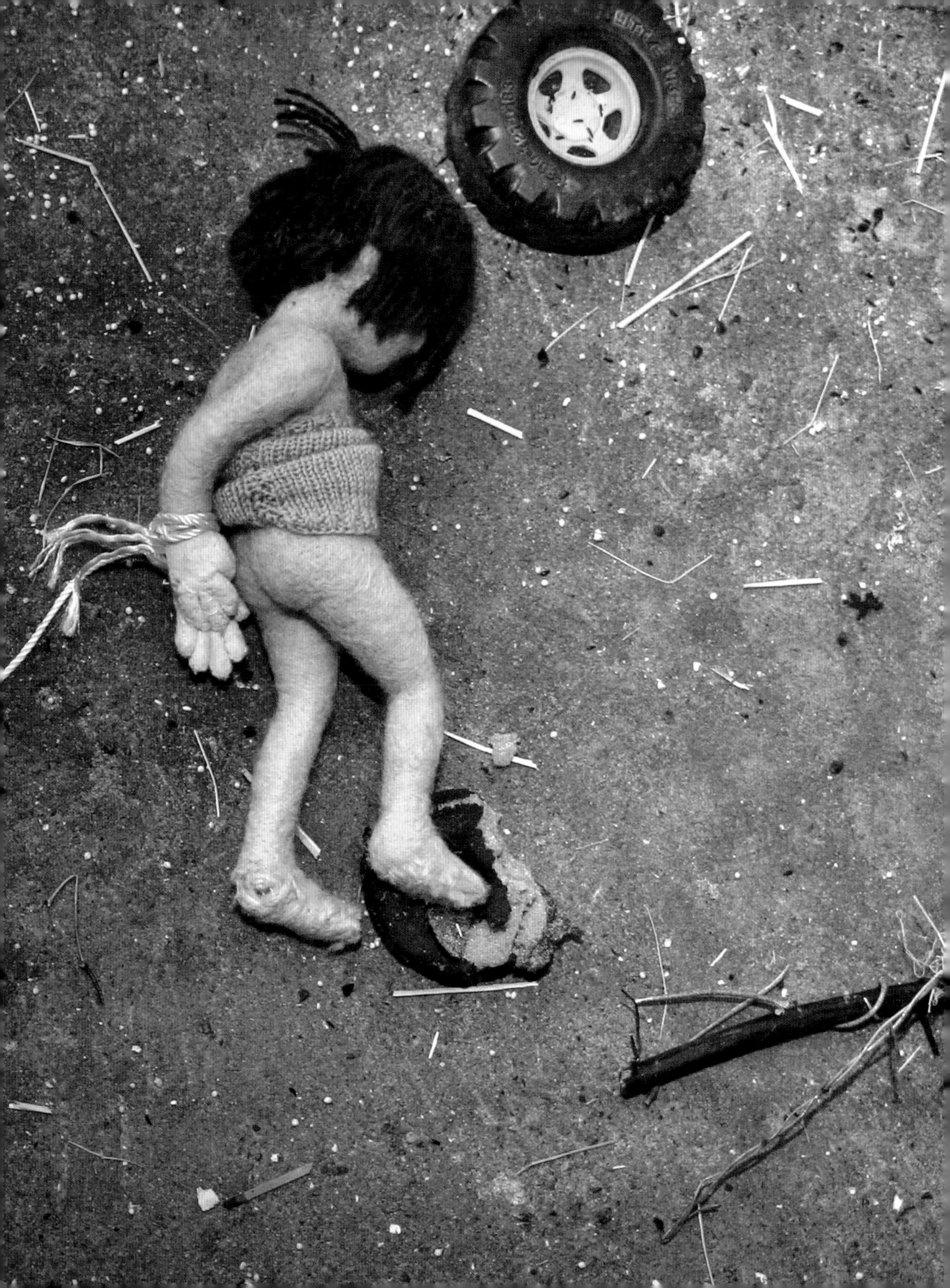

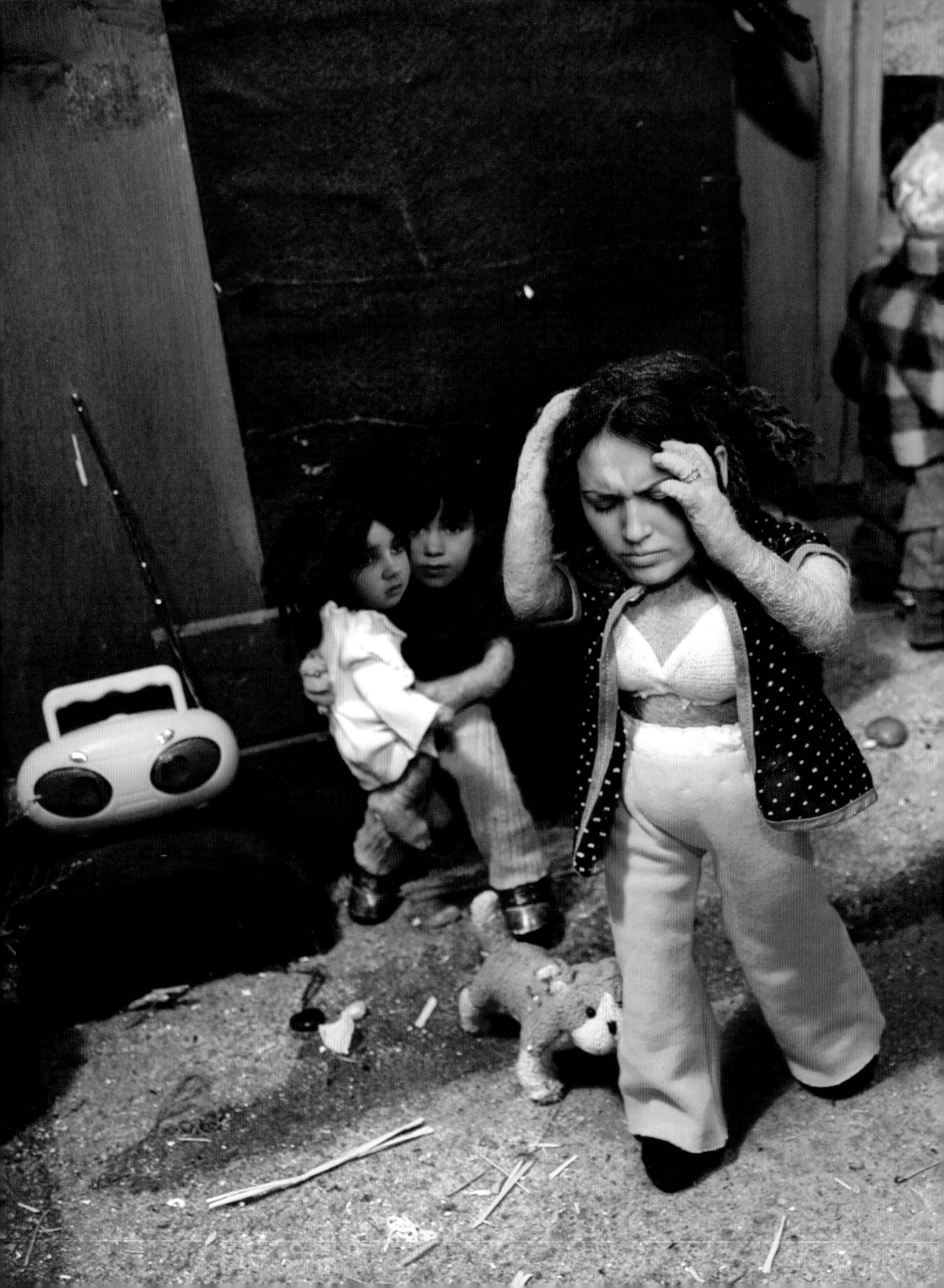

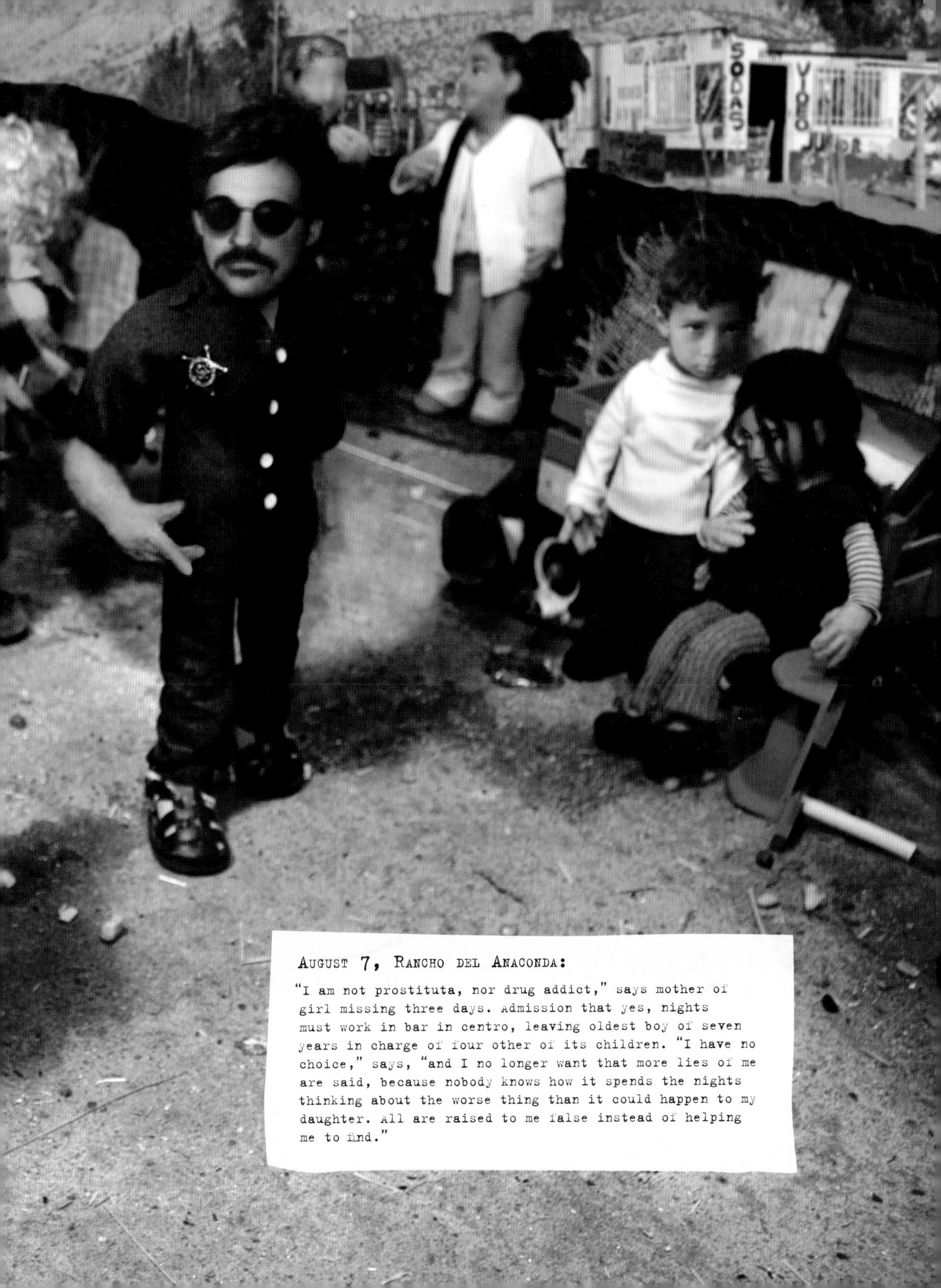
SODAS
VIDEO

August 7, Rancho del Anaconda:

"I am not prostituta, nor drug addict," says mother of girl missing three days. Admission that yes, nights must work in bar in centro, leaving oldest boy of seven years in charge of four other of its children. "I have no choice," says, "and I no longer want that more lies of me are said, because nobody knows how it spends the nights thinking about the worse thing than it could happen to my daughter. All are raised to me false instead of helping me to find."

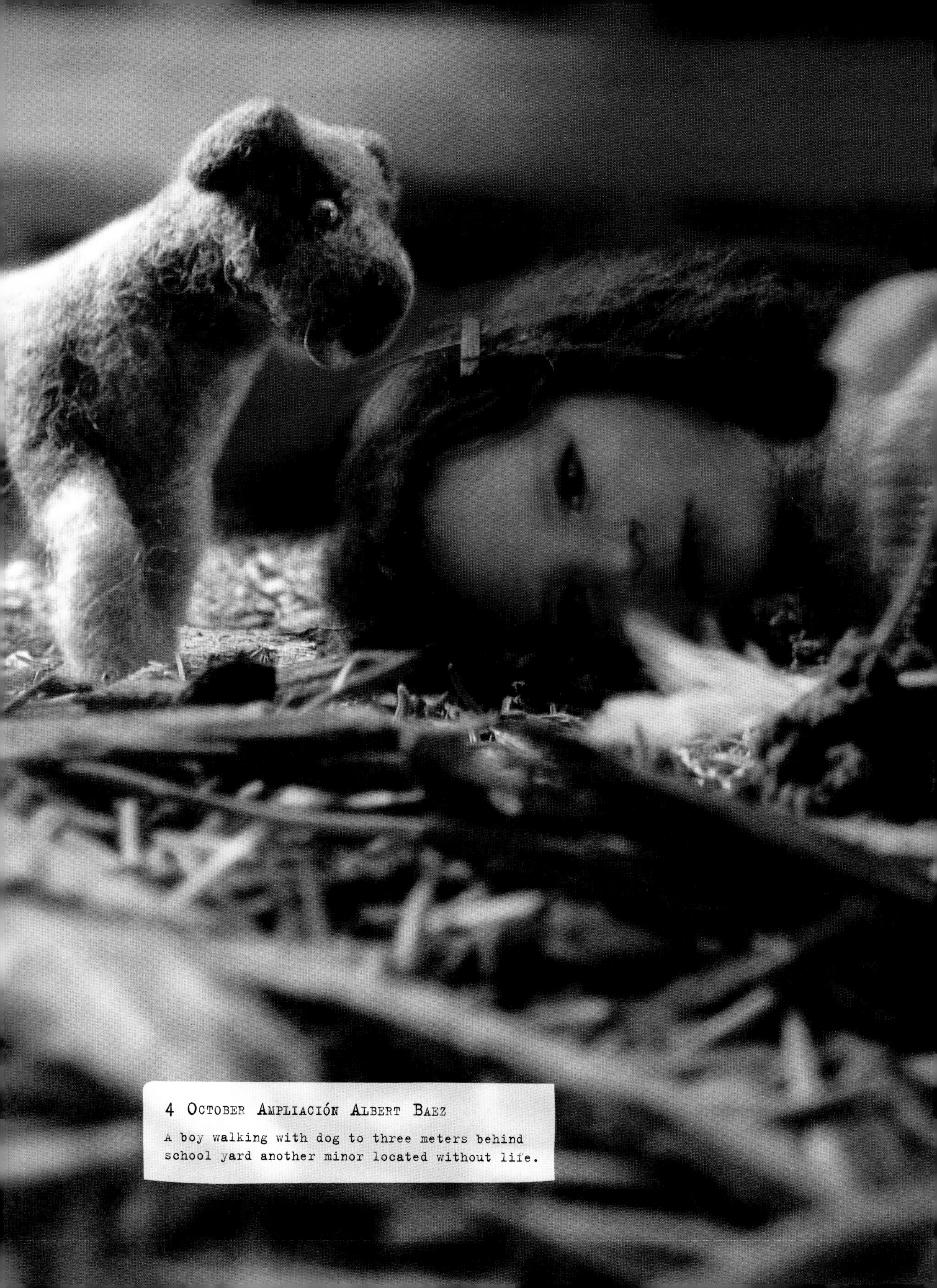

4 October Ampliación Albert Baez

A boy walking with dog to three meters behind school yard another minor located without life.

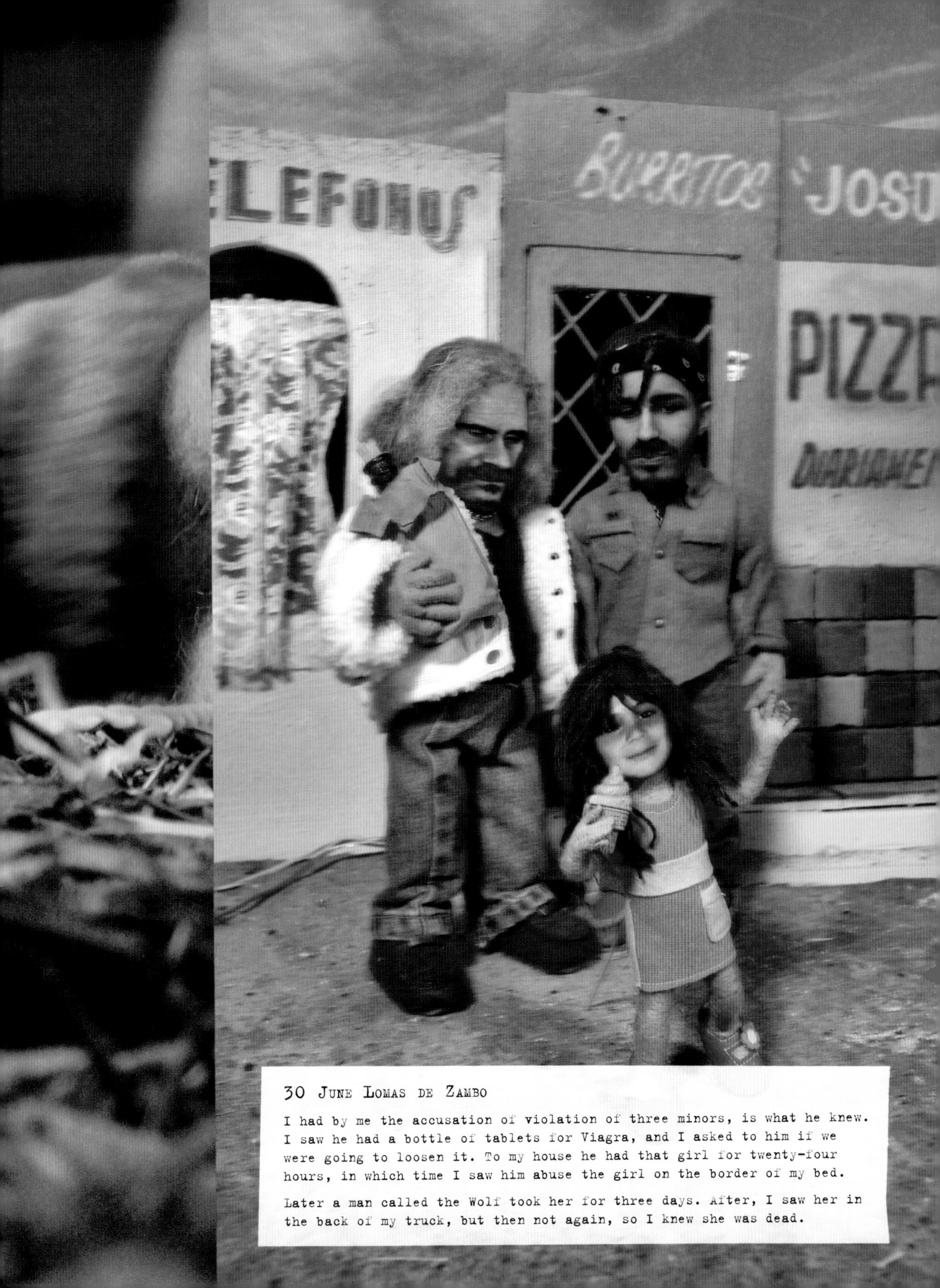

30 June Lomas de Zambo

I had by me the accusation of violation of three minors, is what he knew. I saw he had a bottle of tablets for Viagra, and I asked to him if we were going to loosen it. To my house he had that girl for twenty-four hours, in which time I saw him abuse the girl on the border of my bed.

Later a man called the Wolf took her for three days. After, I saw her in the back of my truck, but then not again, so I knew she was dead.

September 30, Colonia de los Difuntos Valientes

According to this man, it and his pair began to have problems of sentimental character two months ago, due to an infidelity on the part of the woman. "She was going me to leave," said.

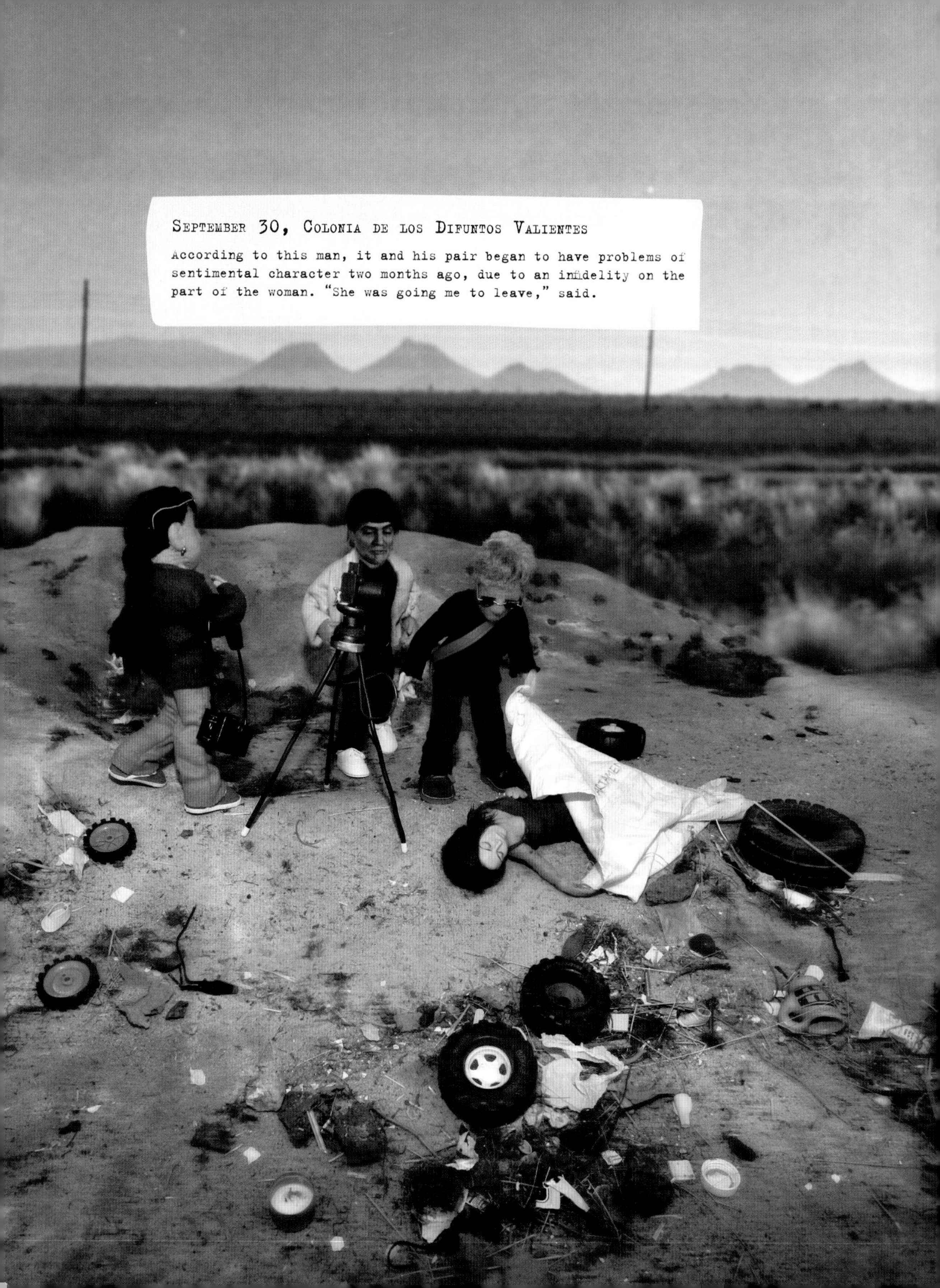